RUDOLF BILLER

EDITORIAL ADVISER: MICHAEL ANKER MHCIMA FCFA

GARNISHING
AND
DECORATION

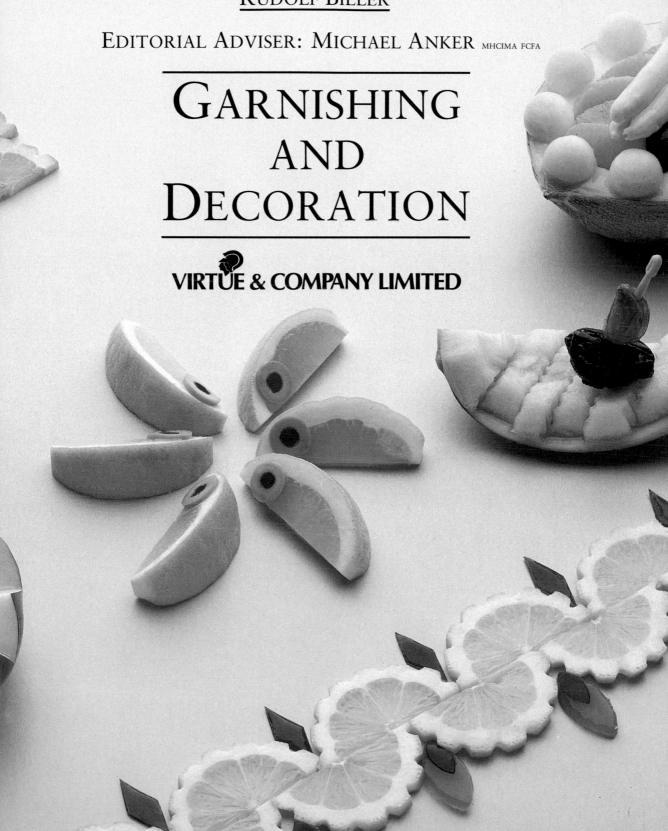

VIRTUE & COMPANY LIMITED

CONTENTS

Foreword	6
A Festive Buffet	8
Savoury Dishes	10
Citrus Fruits	26
Apples, Pears and Peaches	34
Exotic Fruits	40
Tubers and Root Vegetables	50
Onions	61
Fruits used as Vegetables	64
Asparagus, Celery and Globe Artichoke	74
Gourds and Cucumber	80
Mushrooms	90
Bread and Rolls	92
Choux Pastry Goods	94
Butter Garnishes	96
Egg Garnishes	100
Sweet and Savoury Aspic Glazes	106
Cocktail Titbits and Canapés	112
Medallions and Cocktails	116
Napkins and Paper Frills	122
Sweet Decorations	124
Buttercream Decorations	132
Chocolate and other Icings	136
Marzipan	142
Icing Sugar and Cocoa Powder	148
Commercial Cake Decorations	150
Recipes	152
Index	159

FOREWORD

The author, Rudolf Biller, at a presentation of his work.

Eating and drinking are basic needs, but that is not all. They also provide a pleasant occasion for convivial social contact. When the occasion is also a festive one, the food and drink served should be not only satisfying from the culinary point of view, but also appetising and tempting to look at. Even if it is something of a cliché to say that food should be "a feast for the eye", it is none the less true.

The ancient Romans recognised the connection between an elaborately decorated table and the appetite. The classic cuisines of Asia too – those of China and Japan – have for centuries attached enormous importance to garnishes for their dishes. However, for domestic purposes we should bear in mind that the pleasure of eating ought to be greater than that of looking – a guest should be able to help himself without being afraid of destroying a work of art.

Anyone who has once been concerned with the subject of "garnishing and decoration" will not find it difficult to proceed from a small dish to a large buffet. The important thing to bear in mind for a buffet is consistency of style. A festive one should not contain any rustic dishes. The general principle is to arrange the buffet starting from a central eye-catching feature and work towards the corners of the table. All the dishes should be within easy reach. The garnishes and decorations in this book are intended to assist in improving the appearance of dishes for everyday meals and also for festive or other celebratory occasions by means of imaginative, yet classic, decoration.

In addition to working techniques, this book also contains details of the various products used, facilitating the handling of fruit or vegetables, with information on storage and methods of use.

The pages that follow present practical examples of ways in which meat, fish or cheese dishes, and also sweets, may be made to look more attractive by decorating them with fruit, vegetables or creams and icings. Instructions on preparing and working with the various garnishes mentioned and the foodstuffs required to make them will be found in the corresponding chapters. The recipes are set out in alphabetical order at the end of the book.

Equipped with this knowledge, it should not be difficult to use your own imagination to develop the themes presented here as stimulating suggestions.

Rudolf Biller

A Festive Buffet

This buffet can be set up with a combination of commercially produced and home-made foods.

The decorations shown are described in this book and may be easily copied.

Savoury Dishes

Large Fish Dish

A whole salmon is coated with aspic and decorated with tomato leaves, truffle ovals and asparagus. The dish is garnished with a lemon coronet containing a grape; a row of grooved halved lemon slices; another of tomato baskets on grooved cucumber slices, filled with olive shaped vegetable salad; a melon edged with melon balls and filled with horseradish cream; and a lemon basket containing capers.

TROUT DISH

The fish are decorated with flowers made up of stuffed olive slices, egg, leek, radish slices and sprigs of dill. Two asparagus tips with strips of tomato make an attractive alternative decoration.

Additional eye-catching features are carrot twists, a tomato rose, grooved lemon twists and a grooved lemon basket containing olives.

DUCK WITH ORNAMENTAL SKEWER

The duck is dressed on a dish which has been
decorated with flowers under aspic. The water
lily containing a strawberry and the smoked
ham fillet rolls filled with asparagus provide a
decorative garnish on either side of the duck.
Impaled on the skewer are a lemon coronet, an
orange segment and two cocktail cherries, a
tomato coronet, a turned mushroom cap and a
grape.

SAVOURY DISHES

SADDLE OF PORK

The saddle of pork is
decorated with medallions
garnished in three different
ways; stuffed eggs; a tomato
rose in a nest of cress; and half
a sweet pepper filled with
vegetable salad.

SAVOURY DISHES

SADDLE OF VEAL

The slices of veal, arranged on the rib cage, are decorated with green and white asparagus tips together with carrot twists. One end of the dish is garnished with orange baskets containing Waldorf salad, tangerine, cocktail cherry and walnut, the other with melon wedges filled with melon balls and slices of smoked ham fillet each rolled round a grape.

Savoury Dishes

Roast Beef

The slices of roast beef are laid against a sirloin and decorated with vegetable salad. The dish is garnished with small cucumber boats containing vegetable balls, a stuffed white radish (mooli) and cherry tomatoes.

Savoury Dishes

Sausage and Cheese Platters

These are very often suitable for informal social gatherings. The centrepiece of the sausage platter is a cucumber stuffed with spicy pickled vegetables and edged with a row of cucumber balls.

The cheese dish makes its effect by means of the gondola napkin; the radish roses; and the tomato coronet containing cocktail onions. The butter rose and balls heighten the effect.

23

FRUIT SALAD ARRANGEMENT

Any fruit in season may be used for this fruit platter. Each item is carefully peeled and sliced or divided into sections. The fruit is then arranged stepwise on a dish pyramid fashion. The eye-catching feature is a melon half with strawberries.

Citrus Fruits

Lemon and Lime

Lemons and limes may be bought all the year round. Lemons are sold in all food stores, while limes may be found in good greengrocers' shops or a delicatessen. The main countries supplying lemons are Italy (Sicily) and Spain. Limes come from Brazil, Mexico and Ecuador. Lemons and limes are closely related although they differ externally in skin colour and size. Limes are smaller than lemons and have a thin, very green skin.

Orange

The main countries supplying winter oranges are Spain and Israel, also Morocco, Italy and Greece. Summer oranges come principally from South Africa, South America and California. Although there are about 400 varieties of orange, sweet oranges are generally divided into two main groups in the trade: light-coloured ones with pale skin and flesh, and blood oranges having blood-red flesh and sometimes skins of the same colour. Some examples of light-coloured oranges are navels and shamouti or Jaffa oranges. These oranges are available all year, while blood oranges are on sale from December to mid-March.

Tangerine

Tangerines are smaller than oranges and have a very loose skin which is easily removed. When buying fresh ones, the seedless varieties are to be preferred; clementines are particularly recommended. Another type, mandarins, is available canned in the form of segments. These are particularly suitable for use in decoration.

What to Look for when Buying Citrus Fruits

Ripeness   The fruit should have a fresh, taut skin and be quite firm when pressed. A wrinkled skin is not only unsightly for use in decoration, but also indicates lack of freshness. Fruit with any signs of mould is quite unusable.
N.B.   Where limes are concerned a dark green skin is a sign of ripeness.

Treated Fruit

Most citrus fruits (limes are an exception) are specially treated after harvesting to keep them fresh longer and protect them against blue or green mould. The skins are waxed and treated with preservatives. These cannot be removed even by washing in hot water. Only untreated citrus fruits should be selected if the skins are to be used as well as the flesh, but even in this case the fruit should first be washed.

Tools

For making straight cuts in lemons and limes, a small kitchen knife is used. A medium or fairly large one is required for oranges.
A grooving knife is used to make grooving cuts in the skins of oranges and lemons. If the fruit is then sliced, a star pattern is produced. To cut out lemon, lime or orange slices, cutters of eight to ten different sizes are required. If a plain cutter is used, the skin may be easily removed from the flesh by turning the cutter.

CITRUS FRUITS

SLICES

Lemons, oranges and limes are all suitable fruits for slicing as decorations.

GROOVING

The grooving knife is used to make vertical grooving cuts in the whole fruit.

The fruit is then sliced; fairly thick slices are cut if they are to be used flat or on the edge of a glass, but they are cut somewhat thinner for use as twists.

SUBDIVIDED SLICES

Plain or grooved slices may be cut into halves, quarters or eighths.

CUT-OUT SLICES

The fruit is cut into slices about 5–7 mm ($\frac{1}{4}$ in) thick and the pulp is cut away from the skin with a plain or fluted cutter. No skin should be left on the pulp.

FAN

Three or four half slices are arranged one behind another in the form of a fan.

Grooving

Slicing

Subdividing

Cutting away the skin

Cut-out orange slice with melon ball and triangles of truffle

Grooved lemon slices with cherry tomatoes, lozenges of angelica and truffle dots

Orange segments with cocktail cherries and truffle or black garnishing paste

Halved lemon slices with a plain or grooved skin decorated with slices of stuffed olive, lozenges of angelica or melon balls

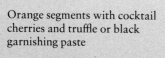

Below, left: Orange slices with crescent-shaped sweet pepper cut-outs and melon balls. Right, above: grooved lemon slice with hearts of sweet pepper

Below: cut-out orange slice with a tomato and angelica flower and ovals of truffle

Lemon fan with lozenges of angelica, a sweet pepper star and a melon ball

CITRUS FRUITS

SLIT SLICES

A plain or grooved slice of citrus fruit is slit as far as the centre. To make a cone, the two ends of a thin slice slit in this way are placed one over another to create a funnel shape. A twist is produced by twisting the two cut surfaces in opposite directions. A number of twists may be arranged one behind another in steps to form a wavy line.

WEDGES

Cut the fruit in half lengthwise, then divide each half into four or five parts.

ORANGE SECTIONS

Cut away the orange or lemon peel at the top and bottom until the pulp is visible. Remove all the peel, cutting close to the pulp, then remove each section separately with a sharp knife.

SLICES WITH A BOW

To decorate a slice with a bow, peel away the skin almost all the way round, then shape the strip of skin into a loose knot. To decorate half a fruit, cut away a 5 mm ($\frac{1}{4}$ in) strip round the top edge, working slightly on a slant, but leaving the strip attached at one point. Shape the strip into a knot.

DECORATION FOR THE RIM OF A GLASS

Cut a lemon into quarters or eighths. Make a cut about 3 cm (1 in) long in the skin, but do not remove the skin. Use this cut to hang the lemon wedge on the rim of a glass.

Sections

Lemon twist and lemon cone

Lemon wedges

Lemon half with bow; below, fan of orange sections

Lemon cone with three cocktail cherries and lozenges of angelica

Fan of three lemon twists on a grooved lemon slice with olive

WATER LILY

Using a pointed knife, slit the skin of an orange or tangerine about eight times from the top about three quarters of the way to the base. Carefully separate the triangles of skin and bend them outwards. Gently detach the orange sections from one another.

Orange flower

Tangerine coronet with cocktail cherry, and various decorations for the rim of a glass

Edging with bow

Lemon cone with tangerine segment, cocktail cherry, lozenge of angelica and walnut; grooved lemon twists

Lemon wedges with slices of stuffed olive

31

CITRUS FRUITS

ORANGE BASKET

Trim off the top and bottom of an orange and cut it in half. Remove the pulp from each half with a spoon. Make grooving cuts in another orange, cut off two thick slices and brush these with dissolved gelatine or with aspic (recipe p. 106). Place one of the orange halves on each slice and line the inside with a little aspic. When this has set the orange halves are watertight and may be filled as desired.

BASKET WITH HANDLE AND PLAIN OR SERRATED EDGE

Using a sharp knife, cut smoothly along the dotted lines as shown to make a handle. Remove the pulp. To make the second basket, cut a band 2 cm (about 1 in) wide above the centre of the fruit, then cut through the fruit in the middle zigzag fashion as far as the base of the handle.

CORONET

Mark the centre of the fruit so that it may be cut evenly. Using a pointed knife, make zigzag cuts right through the middle. Carefully separate the two halves. Cut a thin slice off the base of each one to make it stand firmly. Remove the pulp.

Removing the pulp

Baskets

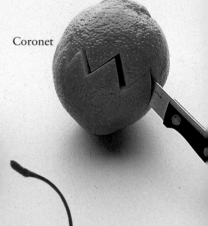

Coronet

Orange basket with plain edge filled with olives

Orange coronet filled with Waldorf salad (see recipe section)

JELLY ORANGES AND LEMONS

Cut the fruit in half lengthwise and carefully remove the pulp with a spoon. Stand the halves on a glass to hold them steady. Pour mint jelly and red-currant jelly (see recipe section) into the fruit halves and leave in the refrigerator to set. Cut into wedges for garnishing.

Jelly orange

Orange basket with serrated edge filled with pickled fruit

Red-currant jelly orange wedges and mint jelly lemon wedges

Grooved orange basket with fruit salad

33

APPLES, PEARS AND PEACHES

APPLE

Apples are grown worldwide in over 20,000 varieties. Nevertheless, the apple is a fruit of temperate zones, for it is only here that it can develop a balance between refreshing acidity and delicious sweetness.

In this country the apple season begins in about August with the early Discovery variety, followed by Worcester Pearmain and James Grieve. Mid to late season varieties include Cox's Orange Pippin followed by Laxton's Superb. Among popular imported varieties are Golden Delicious, Granny Smith, Jonathan and Sturmer Pippin.

APPLES FOR GARNISHING AND DECORATION

As apples quickly turn brown when peeled or cut, they have to be suitably treated before use as a garnish. To prevent discoloration the cut fruit should be either poached (see p. 36) or sprinkled with lemon juice, or alternatively coated with aspic.

PEAR

Pears are grown in more than 5,000 varieties. They fall into two main groups, dessert pears with juicy, sweet white flesh, and cooking pears, which are fairly hard and not juicy. The pear harvest is of short duration as this fruit spoils quickly. For this reason canned pears are often used for culinary purposes, one of the best known varieties being William.

Peach

There are over 2,000 varieties
of peach. The fruit has a
velvety skin and firm, juicy
pulp round a large stone. A
distinction is made between
free-stone peaches, with flesh
that separates easily from the
stone, and cling-stone
peaches, with flesh that is
difficult to remove.
Peaches are available from
April until September. They
are imported during these
months from Italy, Greece
and France. In the winter they
are exported from South
Africa.
Peaches may be successfully
combined with raspberries
and strawberries.

Tools

Apples and pears may be very
thinly pared with a peeler.
The kitchen knife used for
cutting and slicing this type of
acid fruit *must* be made of
stainless steel to prevent
tarnishing.
A special cutter will cut the
fruit into equal parts and core
it at the same time.
Pastry cutters are used to
prepare apples for filling. For
the inside edge a fairly small
one about 3½ to 4 cm (1½ in)
across is used. The one for the
outer edge should be larger,
about 5 to 6 cm (2 to 2½ in)
across, and may be fluted if
desired.
Parisian cutters of various
sizes are used to core or
hollow out apples and pears
intended for stuffing.

APPLES, PEARS AND PEACHES

PEELING APPLES

The peel is cut away spirally with a peeler. A Parisian cutter is used to core apple halves. If small slices are required, a crescent-shaped cut is made with a small knife to remove the core.

POACHING APPLES

Cut the apple as required for the garnish, then poach in white wine flavoured with a little sugar, a stick of cinnamon and a little lemon. Depending on the poaching time the fruit will be either soft or firm to the bite.

COATING APPLES FOR FRYING

Drain the slices, coat with flour and shallow fry in butter until evenly browned. Alternatively, coat the slices with flour, beaten egg and flaked almonds or desiccated coconut. Deep or shallow fry in butter until golden.

Peeling

Coring

POACHED APPLES FOR STUFFING

A small variety such as Cox's Orange Pippin should be used for this purpose, or larger apples may be substituted and trimmed down with a cutter. Various sizes of cutter, either plain or fluted, are required – a larger one for the outside edge, a smaller one for the inside and a Parisian one for coring. Cut round the outside of the apple with the larger cutter. Press the smaller one into the apple to a depth of about 1 cm ($\frac{1}{2}$ in) and remove the core cleanly with the Parisian cutter, taking care not to damage the outer edge. Poach the prepared apples in white wine containing sugar, lemon zest, a clove and a stick of cinnamon.

Poached apple slice

Almond coated apple slice

Coconut coated apple slice

Cut-out apple for stuffing

Above left: apple stuffed with cranberries, edged with almonds and topped with a melon ball; right, apple stuffed with cocktail cherries and lozenges of angelica; below, apple stuffed with chestnut purée (see recipe section), pistachios and chestnut

Poached apple slice with pistachio edging, melon balls and a cocktail cherry; centre, poached apple slice with a slice of kiwi fruit and a prune; left, poached apple slice with chestnut purée (see recipe section), strip almonds and a strawberry

Apple wedges with half-slices of kiwi fruit, prunes and sliced strawberries

37

Apples, Pears and Peaches

Peeling Pears

Pears are peeled downwards with a peeler, starting from the stalk end. The pear is cored in the same way as an apple.

Poached Pear for Stuffing

Peel the pear and cut it in half. Remove the core with a Parisian cutter and poach the halves in white wine containing sugar, a cinnamon stick, cloves and lemon zest. Depending on the poaching time, the fruit will be either fairly soft or firm to the bite. Leave in the wine until cold. Before stuffing, trim the base a little for greater stability.

Hedgehog

Peel the fruit and cut it in half, or use canned pears. Remove the core with a Parisian cutter. Stud the outside of the halves with strip almonds which have been roasted in the oven at 180°C(350°F) until golden brown.

Peeling Peaches

Plunge the peach into boiling water, leave for about half a minute, then plunge into cold water, leave for about three minutes, remove and peel with a pointed knife.

Peeling

Coring

Trimming the base

Pear half stuffed with chestnut purée (see recipe section), a lozenge of angelica, cranberries and a chestnut

Hedgehog

Peeling

Stoning

Stoning Peaches

Starting from the stalk end, cut through the peach all the way round and twist the two halves off the stone.

Peach Segments

Cut each half lengthwise for whole slices and across for half slices. Six wedges are obtained by making three diagonal cuts.

Pear hedgehog

Grooved slice of blood orange with a peach half, strawberries and a melon ball

Pear wedges with a strawberry and pistachios

Peach wedges with cocktail cherries

Peach hedgehog.
The peach halves are studded with roasted strip almonds in the same way as pear hedgehogs.
Canned peach halves may be used.

39

EXOTIC FRUITS

PINEAPPLE

Pineapple is obtainable throughout the year. Because of its versatility, fresh pineapple is a popular table decoration.

The ripeness of a pineapple may be judged by the colour of the skin. The fruit is ripe once its original light orange colour has turned from dark orange to coppery red.

HOW TO STORE PINEAPPLE

Pineapple is a delicate fruit which does not withstand exposure to cold (18°C–64°F is the correct storage temperature) or pressure. The problem of pressure may be solved by tying a piece of strong twine round the base of the leafy top and hanging the pineapple up.

BANANA

The banana is a sweet tropical fruit mostly eaten raw, but it may be used in cookery, especially fried or baked or served *flambé*.

If bananas are to be used in cooking, they should be only just ripe. For eating raw, they should be quite ripe and slightly speckled with brown. Bananas should be stored at room temperature, preferably lightly stacked in a fruit dish. Refrigeration interrupts the ripening process and the fruit tastes bitter.

If they are to be used for garnishing, the peeled fruit and any cut surfaces should be sprinkled with lemon juice to prevent discoloration.

KIWI FRUIT

Kiwi fruit is about the size of an egg. It has a hairy brownish green skin which has to be removed before eating. The flesh is bright green with a slightly lighter centre and contains a ring of small black seeds. It has a slightly acid, fragrant and refreshing taste somewhat reminiscent of gooseberries or melon.

Its fresh colour and decorative appearance makes kiwi fruit very suitable for garnishing and decoration. In addition, it keeps well.

Fresh kiwi fruit may be bought throughout the year. It is ripe if it gives a little when pressed. It will even keep for two or three weeks in the vegetable crisper of the refrigerator.

MELON

There are many varieties of melon. A small selection is given below.

Honeydew   These melons are oval in shape and have a lemon-yellow skin. The flesh is very sweet.

Cantaloup   This is a very sweet melon with flesh of a pale orange colour.

Charentais   Has apricot-coloured flesh and is also very sweet.

Ogen   These are relatively small melons with a yellowish-green skin and very fragrant greenish-white flesh.

WHAT TO LOOK FOR WHEN BUYING MELONS

The ripeness of a melon is not judged by the colour of its skin, but by smell and pressure. A ripe melon smells rather like pineapple and musk. It should yield to slight pressure at the blossom end. Melons should be stored in the vegetable crisper of the refrigerator, where they will keep longer. Apart from this, melon tastes best when well chilled.

TOOLS

Medium size knives are used for peeling and cutting. The cutter is used to core pineapple. By means of the curved grapefruit knife, the pineapple flesh may be cut away from the skin once the fruit has been cut into quarters. The Parisian cutter is required to cut out melon balls and a fancy knife may be used for the decorative trimming of pieces of melon.

41

Exotic Fruits

Peeling Pineapple

Wash the pineapple well and cut off the stalk with a sharp knife. Working from the top down to the stalk end, cut off the skin all round in strips about $1\frac{1}{2}$ cm ($\frac{5}{8}$ in) wide. Remove the "eyes" by means of wedge-shaped cuts, working in a spiral from the top downwards.

Pineapple Pieces

Cut the pineapple into four or six parts from the top to the base. Make a lengthwise cut to remove the core. Cut the flesh off the skin and divide into six or eight small pieces.

Individual Slices

Wash the pineapple and cut into slices about $1\frac{1}{2}$ to 2 cm ($\frac{3}{4}$ in) thick, working from the stalk end. Remove the hard core with a small plain cutter about 2 to $2\frac{1}{2}$ cm (1 in) across. To remove the outside skin select a cutter about $1\frac{1}{2}$ cm ($\frac{5}{8}$ in) smaller than the slices. This will ensure that the "eyes" are cut away with the skin.

Decorated Slices

Decorate the slice of pineapple in the centre or round the edge with berries, cherries, asparagus tips or a cream.

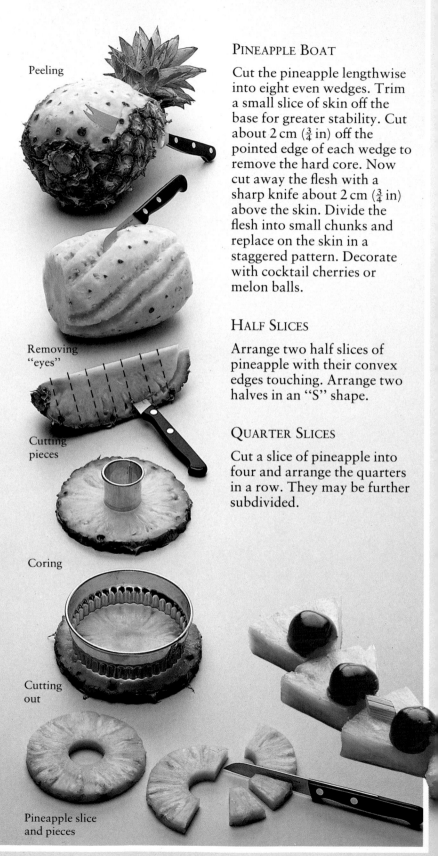

Peeling

Removing "eyes"

Cutting pieces

Coring

Cutting out

Pineapple slice and pieces

Pineapple Boat

Cut the pineapple lengthwise into eight even wedges. Trim a small slice of skin off the base for greater stability. Cut about 2 cm ($\frac{3}{4}$ in) off the pointed edge of each wedge to remove the hard core. Now cut away the flesh with a sharp knife about 2 cm ($\frac{3}{4}$ in) above the skin. Divide the flesh into small chunks and replace on the skin in a staggered pattern. Decorate with cocktail cherries or melon balls.

Half Slices

Arrange two half slices of pineapple with their convex edges touching. Arrange two halves in an "S" shape.

Quarter Slices

Cut a slice of pineapple into four and arrange the quarters in a row. They may be further subdivided.

Pineapple boat with cocktail cherry and melon balls

Pineapple slice with chestnut purée (see recipe section), lozenges of angelica, a slice of pickled walnut and a chestnut

Left, half slices with a strawberry and slices of angelica; right, half slices with truffle crescents arranged in a wavy line

Slice with asparagus, tomato segments and halved pickled walnut (left); right, fig hedgehog on quarter pineapple slices; below, left, eighths with lozenges of angelica and half cocktail cherries

43

EXOTIC FRUITS

ALMOND COATED PINEAPPLE SLICE

Flour a pineapple slice, coat with egg and flaked almonds and deep or shallow fry.

PINEAPPLE SLICE WITH FIG HEDGEHOG

Brown a slice of pineapple quickly in a very hot pan. This will caramelise the sugar in the pineapple and produce a decorative striped pattern. Place half a fresh dark fig on top. Stud it with slivers of roasted strip almonds and surround with lozenges of angelica.

COCONUT COATED PINEAPPLE SLICE

Flour a pineapple slice, coat it with egg and desiccated coconut, then deep fry until brown. Place two tangerine sections on top and decorate with a strawberry and a pistachio nut.

STUFFED PINEAPPLE

Cut a "lid" off a whole pineapple: a lengthwise cut is best for easy removal of the flesh. Now insert a sharp knife into the flesh 2 cm ($\frac{3}{4}$ in) from the edge and run it right round. Scoop out the flesh with a curved grapefruit knife or a spoon. Replace the lid on a slant as a garnish. If necessary, secure it with an ornamental skewer.

N.B. If the pineapple is to be displayed on a slant, the base is trimmed level with a knife and the pineapple is propped against an apple which has had a wedge cut out of it 2 cm ($\frac{3}{4}$ in) thick at one end and about 4 cm ($1\frac{1}{2}$ in) thick at the other.

Propping the pineapple against a suitably cut apple

Cutting

Scooping out the flesh

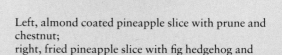

Left, almond coated pineapple slice with prune and chestnut;
right, fried pineapple slice with fig hedgehog and lozenges of angelica

Pineapple split in two lengthwise and filled with fruit salad; below, left, coconut coated fried pineapple slice with tangerine sections, strawberry and pistachio nut; right, half pineapple cut horizontally and filled with stuffed chicken breast (from delicatessen store), sliced kiwi fruit, melon balls and a cocktail cherry with its stalk

45

EXOTIC FRUITS

ROUND BANANA SLICES

Peel the banana and cut across evenly into slices. Arrange these in a row, a circle or a clover leaf pattern.

OVAL BANANA SLICES

Peel the banana and slice obliquely. These slices are larger than round ones and may also be arranged in a fan.

BANANA BOAT

Cut away a strip of peel with a sharp, pointed knife to a depth of about 3 mm ($\frac{1}{8}$ in), leaving one end attached. Roll the strip back to this point. Secure it with a skewer and impale a strawberry or prune on the end. Fill the boat with a sliced banana mixed with dark-coloured fruit.

<u>N.B.</u> Garnishes made with banana should not be prepared until just before serving as the flesh discolours quickly, even when sprinkled with lemon juice.

KIWI SLICES

Kiwi fruit may be sliced lengthwise or across. Peel the fruit and slice evenly. Arrange the slices decoratively one behind another, overlapping them slightly. Alternatively, they may be arranged in a ring surrounding a tomato rose (see p. 67).

KIWI CORONET

Using a pointed knife, cut through the fruit zigzag fashion as far as the middle. Carefully separate the two halves and flatten the base a little.

<u>N.B.</u> Kiwi fruit may be used as a garnish with or without the peel. If unpeeled, the flesh has to be scooped out. This means that dessert spoons should always be provided if unpeeled kiwi fruit garnishes are used.

Round and oval slices

Banana boat

Kiwi slices

Kiwi coronet

Banana slices with pistachios. Bottom, left, banana flower with cocktail cherry; right, kiwi coronet on a cut-out slice of mango with cranberry cream (see recipe section), almond and cocktail cherry.

Oval banana slices with strawberry

Banana boat with fruit salad; below, right, overlapping slices of kiwi fruit; left, half kiwi fruit with cranberry cream (see recipe section), tangerine sections and a walnut; centre, banana slices and kiwi coronet with cranberry cream and grape halves

47

Exotic Fruits

Melon Wedges

Cut the melon along its length into six or eight wedges. Remove the seeds with a tablespoon and cut off the flesh with a curved grapefruit knife. Using a serrated decorating knife, cut the flesh into bite-size pieces, either straight across or obliquely.

Stuffed Melon with Lid

Wash the melon and cut off the top third. Remove the seeds with a tablespoon. Trim the base of the lower half a little for greater stability. Fill as desired. Melons may be filled with strawberries in port wine sabayon, orange sections with strip almonds, pineapple and blackberries, or any other fruit salad. After filling, secure the lid in place with a decorative skewer.

Stuffed Melon with Ball Edging

Cut the melon in half and remove the seeds with a tablespoon. Trim the base of each half for greater stability. Cut out eight balls of melon flesh with a Parisian cutter and arrange evenly round the rim of each melon half. Fill as desired.

Melon Coronet

Cut right through the centre of the melon zigzag fashion with a pointed knife. Gently twist the two halves apart. Remove the seeds with a tablespoon.

Jelly Melon

Cut a fairly small melon in half and remove the seeds with a tablespoon. Stand the melon half on a glass and fill with red-currant jelly (see recipe section). Refrigerate until set, then cut into garnishing slices.

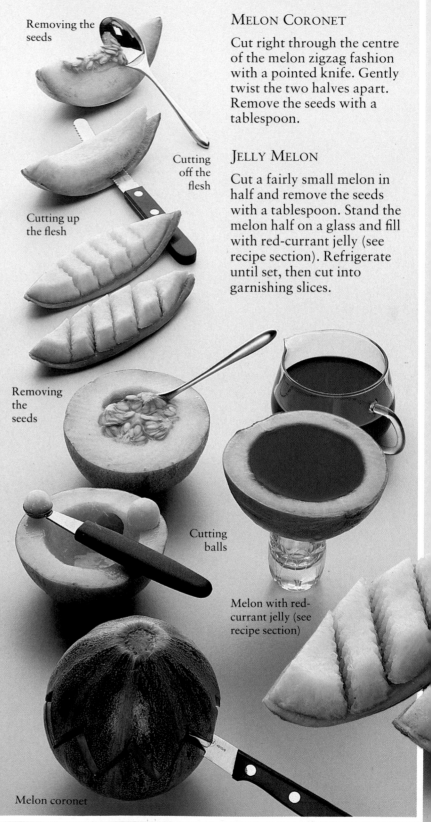

Removing the seeds

Cutting off the flesh

Cutting up the flesh

Removing the seeds

Cutting balls

Melon with red-currant jelly (see recipe section)

Melon coronet

Left, melon with ball edging filled with exotic fruit salad; right, melon coronet and strawberries; below, left, slices of jelly melon

Left, melon boat with cocktail cherry and mandarin segment; right, melon filled with Waldorf salad, orange sections, a walnut and a cocktail cherry. The skewer is decorated with cherry tomatoes. The base consists of a slice of melon with small tomato cut-outs.

TUBERS AND ROOT VEGETABLES

POTATOES

There are at present some 100 varieties of potato. There are marked differences between some of them as regards appearance, taste and cooking qualities. For this reason, they may be divided into three groups according to their cooking qualities:

Waxy varieties with a close texture which remain firm when cooked – these are suitable for salads and for frying.

Firm-cooking varieties particularly suitable for boiling, either peeled or in their skins.

Floury, firm-cooking varieties, mainly suitable for mashing.

HOW TO STORE POTATOES

Storage in a cool, dark and airy place is essential; a cellar is the most suitable. The potatoes should be placed on slatted wooden shelving for storage. The tubers must be firm-skinned, dry and unblemished; all those showing any damage should be discarded and the remainder should be regularly inspected. If no suitable cellar is available, every effort should be made to provide dark, dry storage conditions.

N.B. Potatoes sold in a plastic pack *must* be removed from their wrapping as soon as they are brought home to prevent deterioration.

CELERIAC

Celeriac is on sale for most of the year. The main season is from October to April. Fresh celeriac is hard and free from dark patches. If it sounds hollow when tapped and feels relatively light, it is old and spongy inside. Before use it should be lightly scrubbed under running water, any roots and green parts being removed at the same time. Celeriac discolours quickly once it has been cut. This may be prevented by adding lemon juice to the water in which it is cooked. Celeriac may be stored whole for about a week in the vegetable crisper of the refrigerator.

CARROT

Fresh carrots are obtainable throughout the year, but the supply is best and cheapest in the autumn. They may sometimes be bought in bunches with their leafy tops and will remain freshest if the tops are not removed until shortly before use. Cool, dry storage is required.

CLEANING CARROTS

New carrots merely require scrubbing with a hard brush. Old ones should be thinly pared with a peeler.

RADISHES

Red radishes and white radishes (mooli) are on sale throughout the year. There is also a black variety of large radish similar to mooli. Red radishes belong to the same family, of which they are a dwarf variety. These are milder in the springtime. When buying radishes, care should be taken to select firm ones only, rejecting any which are split or spongy.

TOOLS

Savoy bag for piping potato shapes; Parisian and various other cutters for carrots and celeriac. The knives are required for decorative cutting and trimming. The corkscrew type cutter is used for cutting spirals.

51

TUBERS AND ROOT VEGETABLES

POTATO MIXTURE FOR DECORATIONS (DUCHESSE)

Peel the potatoes, boil them and press through a ricer. If they are too watery after cooking, dry them well on a baking tray in the oven at 160°C (320°F). Mix the purée with egg yolk, using three yolks for 1 kg (2¼ lb) potatoes. Season with salt and a little grated nutmeg. Shape into cylinders about 2½ cm (1 in) across and place on a floured slab, or pipe out with a savoy bag without a tube and dust lightly with flour. Cut the cylinders to the required size (for croquettes, balls, pear or cakes).

Ingredients for potato mixture

Crumbing

Coating with almonds

Various potato shapes

DEEP FRIED POTATO GARNISHES

CROQUETTES

Cut the piped potato mixture into cylinders about 5 cm (2 in) long. Dust with flour, egg and crumb, and deep fry at 170–180°C (340–350°F).

POTATO BALLS

Cut the piped potato mixture into 2½ to 3 cm (about 1 in) lengths and roll each one into a ball. Egg and crumb them and deep fry at 170–180°C (340–350°F).

ALMOND BALLS

Prepare in the same way as potato balls, but coat with egg and flaked almonds. Deep fry at 170–180°C (340–350°F).

POTATO PEAR

Mould about 80 to 100 g (3 oz) potato mixture between the hands to the shape of a pear, then egg and crumb. A piece of spaghetti is used for the stalk and a bay leaf may be inserted at the side. Deep fry at 170–180°C (340–350°F).

"BETHMÄNNCHEN" POTATOES

Shape the potato mixture into small balls, wash with beaten egg yolk, decorate with three split almonds and deep fry at 170–180°C (340–350°F).

Top, potato balls and potato pears;
below, almond balls and
"Bethmännchen" potatoes;
right, potato croquettes

53

Tubers and Root Vegetables

Shallow Fried Potato Garnishes

Potato and Cheese Cakes

Mix 500 g (1 lb) prepared potato mixture with about 50 g (2 oz) grated Emmental or Parmesan cheese as desired. Shape into cylinders about 5 cm (2 in) across, allow to cool, then cut in slices 1½ to 2 cm (about ¾ in) thick. Dust with flour and reshape a little. Shallow fry over moderate heat until golden brown. Using a tablespoon, decorate the top with a pile of diced onions which have been browned in butter. Sprinkle with chopped parsley. Before frying, the cakes may be decorated with a diamond pattern, using the back of a knife.

Potato and Bacon Cakes

Finely dice about 50 g (2 oz) bacon and 50 g (2 oz) onion. Fry the bacon in a frying pan until lightly browned, then add the onion and fry until transparent. Stir into 500 g (1 lb) potato mixture and add a little freshly chopped parsley. Shape the mixture into rolls about 5 cm (2 in) thick, allow to cool, then cut in slices 1½ to 2 cm (about ¾ in) thick. Dust with a little flour and reshape slightly. Mark a pattern on top with the back of a knife and shallow fry over moderate heat until golden brown.

Potato Sausages

Roll about 60 g (2 oz) potato mixture into a ball. Dust with a little flour and shape into sausages. Flatten a little and shallow fry over moderate heat until golden brown.

Baked Potato Garnishes

Potato and Cheese Buns

Mix the potato mixture with bacon and onions or diced ham or parsley and onions. Pipe on to a working surface and shape into balls 3½ cm (about 1½ in) across. Flatten a little and wash with beaten egg yolk. Sprinkle the tops with equal amounts of grated Emmental and Parmesan cheese. Transfer to a greased and floured baking sheet and bake at 200°C (390°F) until golden brown.

Duchesse Potatoes

Using a savoy bag and star tube, pipe out the mixture in rosettes on to a buttered and floured baking sheet. Brush the tops with melted butter or with egg yolk and bake at 180–200°C (350–390°F) until golden brown.

Moulded Potatoes

Anna Potatoes

Grease a small tapering round or oval mould with clarified butter and line with potato slices about 2½ to 3 mm (⅛ in) thick. For an attractive pattern, use potatoes which measure the same across as the height of the mould. If necessary, cut the slices to the right size with a cutter. Season the slices with salt and pepper, press them lightly against the edge of the mould and fill with clarified butter. Stand the moulds on a baking sheet and bake at about 200°C (390°F). To test whether the potatoes are cooked, squeeze the edge of a slice gently; if it can be squashed a little and just begins to break up, the potatoes are ready. Briskly invert the moulds on to a wire rack and drain off the surplus clarified butter.

Lined potato mould

Piped potato rosette

Top left, Anna potatoes; right, Duchesse potatoes; centre, potato and cheese buns, potato sausages; below, left, potato and cheese cakes; right, potato and bacon cakes

TUBERS AND ROOT VEGETABLES

GARNISHES USING WHOLE ROOT VEGETABLES

CARROT

Wash and peel a small carrot with a leafy top. Cut off the top, but leave about 4 cm (1½ in) in place. Scrape away any black areas with the point of a knife and clean out the stalk end well.

RADISH

Wash the radishes well and cut off the root end. Remove the outer leaves, retaining only the best inside ones.
N.B. Sand tends to lodge in the stalk. Scrape it out with the point of a knife.

WHITE RADISH (MOOLI)

Clean a small white radish, leaving the best leaves in place. Wash it and peel evenly with a vegetable peeler. Place in cold water to prevent wilting.

RADISH FLOWER HEADS

Rose: make cuts all the way round to divide the radish into 5 petals with 5 smaller ones in between. Remove the root end with a circular cut.
Blossom: make small petals by cutting down into the radish all the way round at intervals of about 3 mm (⅛ in).
Bud: make 4 lengthwise and 6 crosswise incisions running beyond the middle of the radish.
Marguerite: make 12 slashes all round the radish almost as far down as the stalk end. Using the tip of a knife, detach the petals from the white heart of the radish, but leave the lower ends attached.
Coronet: starting from the centre of the radish, run a small pointed knife through it zigzag fashion. The two halves are easily separated.
Water lily: using a grooving knife, make 8 incisions from the top downwards.
Fan: starting at the top of the radish, make 6 straight vertical cuts and place a slice of radish in each space.
N.B. Once the cuts have been made, the radishes will open if left in cold water, preferably containing ice cubes.

RADISH FLOWER

Cut a small radish into slices and arrange these in a ring to make a flower. Place a carrot cut-out in the centre. Cut the stem and leaves from cucumber peel or braised leek.

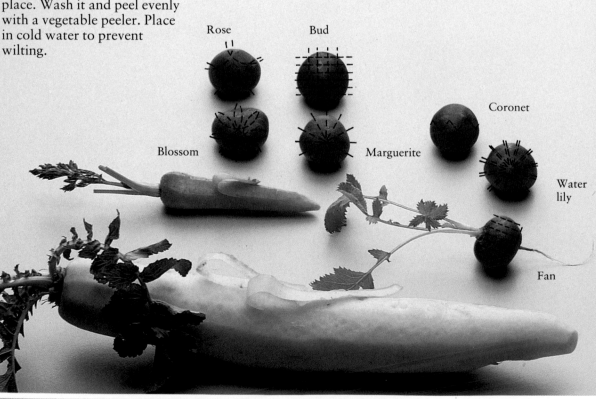

Rose

Bud

Coronet

Blossom

Marguerite

Water lily

Fan

Rose

Blossom

Marguerite

Bud

Coronet

Water lily

Radish flower

Top, white radish, red radishes and carrots with
leafy tops; below, various radish decorations

Fan

57

TUBERS AND ROOT VEGETABLES

CUT-OUT SHAPES

BALLS

Wash and peel the carrot or celeriac. Press an olive or round-shaped Parisian cutter on to it and turn it on its axis under even pressure. Cook the balls in salted water, keeping them firm to the bite.

STARS AND FLOWERS

Cook the carrot or celeriac and slice it. Stamp out fancy shapes with cutters (star, crescent, rosette, heart) and arrange decoratively.

GROOVED SHAPES

Select choice carrots and cook them. Groove them lengthwise with a grooving knife and cut them into slices. Leave these whole or cut them in half before arranging in a row.

TURNED SHAPES

Wash and peel a thick carrot or celeriac. As peeled celeriac discolours after a time it should be sprinkled with lemon juice or vinegar.

WEDGES

Cook the carrot after washing and peeling, then cut in half lengthwise. Cut into wedges by slanting the knife alternately towards the left and the right. Arrange the wedges in a row to provide a decorative edging.

BOATS

Cut the carrot into cylinders 4 to 4½ cm (about 1½ in) long. Cut these lengthwise into quarters.

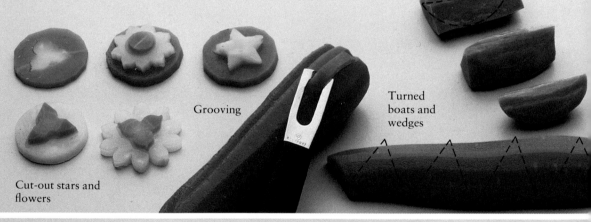

Grooving

Turned boats and wedges

Cut-out stars and flowers

Cut-out shapes

Olive shaped and round decorations

OVALS

Cut the carrot or celeriac into cylinders or chunks 4 to 4½ cm (about 1½ in) long and about 3 cm (1¼ in) across. Now make eight even cuts from end to end. Crescent shaped cuts are first made at the front and back, then on the left and right sides. The next four crescent cuts are made at the four corners.

Turned ovals

Turned and cut-out shapes arranged to make individual patterns

Cut-out, grooved and turned shapes in rows

59

Tubers and Root Vegetables

Stuffed White Radish

Clean the white radish and leave the best leaves in place, then peel it and make an oval cut to hollow it out. Scoop out the flesh with a Parisian spoon. Use the radish balls together with radishes and gherkins to fill the oval. Flatten the base of the radish a little for greater stability.

Carrot Spiral

Cook a carrot and cut it in half crosswise. Insert the special spiral cutter and turn it. The more it is turned, the longer the spiral.

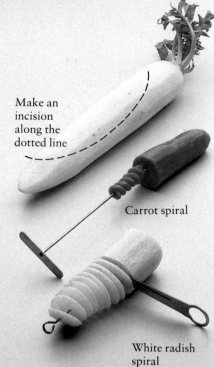

Make an incision along the dotted line

Carrot spiral

White radish spiral

White Radish Spiral

Wash and peel the radish. Trim level the roots at the top and base. Using a corkscrew type spiral cutter, insert its prong into the top of the radish. Turn the cutter evenly to produce a neat spiral. <u>N.B.</u> If left in cold water for a time, the spiral will open well. Pull the ends apart and arrange as a garland or circle.

White radish with gherkins, small corn cobs, olives, carrot balls, silverskin onions and half quails' eggs; below, carrot spirals and radish spiral with red radish rose

Onions

Button Onion

These small, round, marble-size onions are also known as silverskin onions.

Spring Onion (Scallion (U.S.))

Both the elongated white bulbs and the green leaves are eaten. They are used fresh for garnishing and in hors d'oeuvre and salads.

All-Purpose Onion

These are medium-size yellow-skinned onions which keep well and may be used for most purposes.

Shallot

Shallots are small and oval. They are considered the best for flavouring.

Spanish Onion

These are as large as an apple and mild. They are suitable for stuffing and eating raw.

White Onion

These onions are popular for salads as their flavour is not very strong.

Red Onion

This is a mild, spicy variety suitable for eating raw.

How to Store Onions

When buying onions, care should be taken to select those which arc ripe, well-rounded and dry. They should not have begun to sprout and should not feel soft. The best way of storing onions is in nets (never plastic bags) in an airy, cool, dry place. On no account should they be kept in a refrigerator.

Tools

A vegetable knife is used to cut up onions as required.

Onions

Onion Rings

Spanish onions are the most suitable for garnishing. They are used raw for this purpose. Peel an onion, cut off slices and separate these into rings. Colour them by pressing them into paprika, chopped parsley or finely cut chives.
To make a garnish, arrange a red (paprika) ring, a green one (parsley or chives) and a plain one in a row.
<u>N.B.</u> If the parsley or chives will not stick to the rings, these should be brushed with egg white or dissolved aspic jelly.

Onion Flower

Peel a large red onion and a Spanish onion (about 8 cm–3½ in – across) and cut ½ cm (¼ in) slice off the white Spanish onion. Remove the large outer ring.
Cut the red onion lengthwise into quarters and remove 5 or 6 leaves from the base. Cut the bottom of each leaf straight and cut a triangular notch in the tip. Arrange the red leaves round the inside edge of the white Spanish onion ring to overlap slightly. Finish off the onion flower by decorating the centre with cress or parsley or alternatively red radishes or a turned mushroom cap.

Cutting slices

Making rings

A whole slice

Onion coronet and onion flower

Above, onion flower with cress nest and radish rose; above right, Spanish onion slices with pieces of red onion and leek triangles; far right, onion coronet with radish roses.

Below, onion rings with paprika and herbs; foot of page, onion boats with silverskin onions, and onion coronet with vegetable balls.

FRUITS USED AS VEGETABLES

TOMATO

Tomatoes are available all the year round. They include green ones, olivette tomatoes, ribbed beef tomatoes and cherry tomatoes. In addition, red and green ones are sold canned.

Tomatoes have a particularly good flavour if they have ripened outdoors in the sun. They have a more aromatic taste than hothouse ones.

N.B. Tomatoes need warmth not only while growing and when they are harvested, but also in the kitchen. Consequently they should not be stored in a refrigerator, for this causes cell breakdown, resulting in blemishes where rot sets in.

CAPSICUM

There are sweet and hot varieties of capsicum of different sizes and colours. Sweet peppers are very suitable for eating raw, but may also be cooked. The hot types of capsicum or "chillis" are almost solely used as a spice.

Peppers and chillis may be bought fresh all the year round. They are also sold in cans.

AUBERGINE

Aubergines are available all the year round. They are mainly imported from Italy and Spain in the summer, and from Israel and North African countries in the winter and spring.

There are various sizes and shapes. The fruit may vary in colour from dark purple to white. It is not palatable raw, but only develops its nutty flavour after frying or grilling.

Avocado

Avocados are harvested and marketed while still hard. They only develop their full flavour when they are ripe, with flesh of a creamy consistency and a mild, creamy taste. They should therefore be left to ripen at room temperature for a few days (about two to eight) before use. Wrapped in newspaper and stored in a warm place, they will ripen within two or three days. When ripe they may be stored for a few days in the vegetable compartment of a refrigerator.

An avocado is ripe if the flesh yields to gentle pressure, with the exception of the "Hass" variety which has a particularly hard skin and is ripe when the colour has changed from dark green to almost black.

Avocados in Cooking

Avocados are very versatile. They are a suitable ingredient for sweet and savoury salads alike, and may be made into spicy sauces as well as sweet creams. They are also good to eat as they are, with the addition of a little salt, pepper and lemon juice. They should not be cut until just before eating, then sprinkled with lemon juice right away to prevent the flesh from turning brown.

N.B. If avocados are cooked they take on a bitter flavour.

Tools

Fruits used as vegetables may be peeled or cut up with knives of various sizes. A variety of cutters are used for sweet pepper decorations.

Fruits used as Vegetables

Cherry Tomato Garnishes

Cherry or cocktail tomatoes are skinned in exactly the same way as the larger ones. They may be used skinned or unskinned to surround a prepared dish or as general decoration.

Cherry Tomato and Quail's Egg

Cut a cherry tomato in half and scoop out the centre. Stuff it with half a boiled quail's egg, or use half an olive instead.

Skinning Tomatoes

Use a firm tomato. Make a circular cut to remove the stalk. Lightly cut a cross in the skin at the top. Plunge the tomato into boiling water for about 12 to 14 seconds until the skin comes away. Remove and plunge at once into cold water; the skin can now be pulled off easily.

Tomato Half for Stuffing

Cut a skinned tomato in half lengthwise (from the blossom to the stalk end). Scoop out the seeds with a teaspoon or Parisian cutter. Trim the base level for greater stability. Depending on how it is to be used, the tomato half may be stood on a fairly thick slice of cucumber.

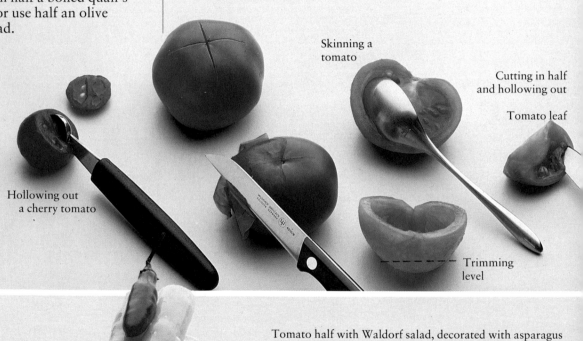

Hollowing out a cherry tomato

Skinning a tomato

Cutting in half and hollowing out

Tomato leaf

Trimming level

Tomato half with Waldorf salad, decorated with asparagus and sweet pepper, on a grooved cucumber slice

Right-hand page
Top, tomato segments with red radish coronet and quail's egg.
Centre, tomato half filled with silverskin onions, cucumber balls, carrot balls and strips of leek on a grooved cucumber slice; right, tomato rose on a bed of cress.
Below, tomato rose on a grooved cucumber slice; centre right, cherry tomato with quail's egg; far right, cherry tomato filled with cheese cream and capers on a red radish coronet.

TOMATO LEAF

Cut an unskinned tomato evenly into six or eight. Remove the seeds and central pulp from each of these triangles. They may be stuffed or arranged in any pattern.

TOMATO ROSE

Using a sharp knife, peel a choice red tomato in a spiral strip 1½–2 cm (about ¾ in) wide. Roll up the strip tightly to begin with, then more loosely at the other end. Use as a garnish.

Tomato rose

Fruits used as Vegetables

Tomato Slices

Without skinning the tomato, slice it evenly with a very sharp knife at right angles to the stalk end.

Tomato Flower

Without skinning the tomato, make 6 or 8 lateral incisions. Fill the spaces with grooved cucumber slices.

Tomato and Egg Domes

Cut the tomato and a hard boiled egg into six even parts.

Arrange the segments alternately to form domes.

Toadstool

Without skinning, flatten the tomato slightly at the stalk end and cut off a lid at the top end. Scoop out the flesh and seeds and fill with vegetable salad. Replace the lid and dot with mayonnaise, using a savoy bag fitted with a plain tube.

Tomato Basket

Cut the top of an unskinned tomato to leave a handle. Scoop out the flesh and seeds with a teaspoon or Parisian cutter. Fill the basket as desired.

Tomato Coronet

Cut right through to the centre of the tomato zigzag fashion. Lightly twist the two halves apart. Flatten the base of each one a little with a knife for greater stability. Depending on use, the tomato halves may be stood on a grooved cucumber slice.

Tomato slices

Tomato wedges

Tomato basket

Lateral incisions

Hollowing out

Tomato coronet

Left, tomato slices with sliced egg and pepper cut-outs; right, tomato coronet with red radish salad and a slice of egg.

Above left, tomato basket with vegetable balls and cress on a grooved cucumber slice; right, tomato flower with grooved cucumber slices and a radish rose. Centre, tomato segments with eggs and a turned mushroom cap. Below, tomato and egg dome, and toadstool with Waldorf salad (see recipe section).

69

FRUITS USED AS VEGETABLES

PREPARING SWEET PEPPERS

Wash the pepper and cut off a fairly thick slice from the stalk end. Now the visible pithy partitions and seeds may be removed with a small knife. After preparing in this way, the pepper may be sliced across or cut into lengthwise strips, or cut in half lengthwise and used to make all kinds of fancy cut-outs.

PEPPERS FOR STUFFING

Cut off the top to make a lid and remove the seeds. Flatten the base a little for greater stability. If the pepper is no longer leakproof once this has been done, a slice of cucumber cut lengthwise or a cut-out slice of celeriac and a little aspic may be used to strengthen the base.

PEPPER RINGS

Cut the pepper into thin rings, either with a knife or with a slicer, which gives a more even result. Arrange the rings one behind another.

Hollowing out a pepper

Cutting into rings

Cutting out

Decorative shapes stamped out of red and green peppers, decorated with mayonnaise and green peppercorns as well as pepper rings

70

Pepper cut in half crosswise and filled with vegetable balls and yoghurt; right, pepper cut in half lengthwise and filled with button mushrooms, celery, avocado slices, tomato wedges and sliced stuffed olives

Fruit used as Vegetables

Aubergines for Stuffing

At first sight aubergines do not seem very suitable for cold garnishes, yet their deep colour provides fine contrasts for a decoration. They are suitable for filling with vegetables, fruit and thick sauces.

To prepare for stuffing, cut the aubergine in half lengthwise and flatten the base a little for greater stability. If the aubergine half is to be stuffed with vegetables or filled with a thick sauce, it will have to be hollowed out first.

Hollowing out an aubergine

Avocados for Stuffing

An avocado contains a large stone. To remove it, the fruit is cut in half lengthwise and the two halves are twisted apart. If one of them is to be stored, the stone should not be removed. Sprinkle the flesh with a little lemon juice to prevent discoloration. Flatten the base of each half a little for greater stability. Also trim off a small slice at the stalk end.

Removing the stone

Avocado Sections

Cut an avocado in half and remove the stone. Pare off the peel (this is easily done if the fruit is ripe) and cut lengthwise into sections as thick as a finger. Sprinkle these with lemon juice and season with salt and freshly ground pepper (black). Arrange them in a fan.

Peeling

Avocado sections

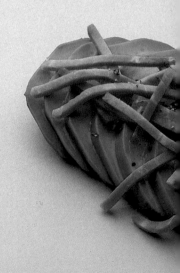

Aubergine with sliced egg, tomato wedges, celery and strips of truffle; right, avocado with boletis mushroom salad; far right, avocado with shrimp and vegetable salad and cream; below, avocado sections with ham salad; right, avocado sections with egg, asparagus, sweet pepper and tomato dots

ASPARAGUS, CELERY AND GLOBE ARTICHOKE

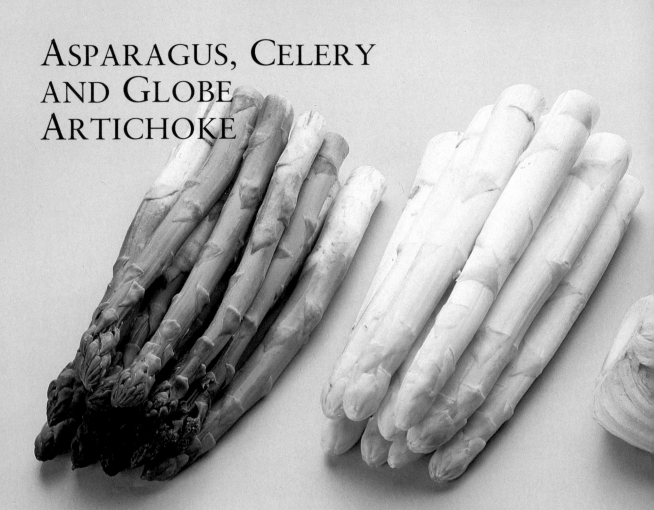

ASPARAGUS

There are white and green varieties of asparagus. The difference between them is not confined to colour; green asparagus grows above ground and has a strong flavour. The asparagus season lasts from early May until the end of June. Asparagus should always be eaten very fresh. The ends should be smooth, well-rounded and juicy; if one spear is struck against another, a tapping sound indicates freshness.

N.B. If asparagus is not used on the same day, it should be washed, wrapped in a damp cloth and stored in the vegetable compartment of the refrigerator.

CELERY

Celery may be bought all the year round. Freshness is essential. Heads with yellowish stalks and wilted leaves should not be used. Fresh celery will keep for about ten days in the vegetable crisper of the refrigerator.

CELERY IN COOKING

To prepare celery the stalks
are first cut off the base, then
the leaves are removed (they
may be used for flavouring)
and the cut end is trimmed. In
addition, the thick outer
stalks may be "strung" in the
same way as rhubarb.

GLOBE ARTICHOKE

Globe artichokes are
harvested as a winter
vegetable in southern Europe
and throughout the year in
America. Very small ones may
be preserved whole; the
delicate hearts and bottoms of
larger ones may also be
bought preserved.
Artichokes are very versatile.
They taste good fried, boiled,
stuffed or "straight" with
various dips and sauces.

TOOLS

The knives are required for
trimming globe artichokes as
well as asparagus spears and
celery stalks. An asparagus, or
other vegetable, peeler is used
for peeling the spears and
stalks.

Asparagus, Celery and Globe Artichoke

Peeling and Cooking Asparagus

Lay the asparagus spear along the left (or right) forearm and grasp the tip between the thumb and second finger. Starting about 3 to 4 cm (1½ in) below the tip, peel the spear smoothly as far as its base while turning it with the thumb and second finger. Use a special asparagus peeler or a vegetable peeler. Place the asparagus in a pan of cold water and add a little salt. If desired, a little monosodium glutamate may also be added to bring out the flavour. Bring the water to the boil and cook the asparagus for exactly five minutes, then remove the pan from the heat and let the asparagus stand for 20 minutes.

N.B. After peeling, trim off about 1 cm (½ in) at the end of each spear. This is very important, as asparagus is often cut with knives which are not stainless, resulting in oxidation at the base of the spear with consequent discoloration during cooking and impairment of the flavour.

Celery

Separate the individual stalks and wash well. Scrape lightly with a peeler and "string" each stalk, then peel again if necessary. Cook gently in a little salted water or vegetable stock until tender. Arrange the stalks on a dish and decorate with fresh, finely cut vegetables. Alternatively, trim the stalks down evenly into 5 to 6 cm (about 2 in) lengths and arrange in small bundles. Wrap each of these in a slice of smoked ham fillet. Another alternative is to cut the stalks into 8 cm (3½ in) lengths, assemble them in bundles and wrap each of these in a slice of smoked goose breast.

Celery in a Goblet

Clean and wash the celery, season it with salt and pepper, and arrange uncooked in a goblet.

Peeling asparagus

Peeling celery

Cooked celery with tomato segments, olives, mushrooms and onions

White asparagus
with ham and
Hollandaise sauce
(see recipe section)

Raw celery in a goblet

Green asparagus with
raw ham (Parma style),
sliced egg, tomato wedges
and sliced olives,
garnished with a turned
mushroom cap in cress
salad

White asparagus spears
with fruit salad and
walnuts

Asparagus, Celery and Globe Artichoke

Preparing and Cooking Globe Artichokes

Artichokes have a long stalk at their base. To remove it, the artichoke is held against the edge of a table with the left (or right) hand and the stalk is broken off under firm pressure with the other hand. The thick threads in the artichoke bottom will be pulled out at the same time. Trim the base a little with a knife to straighten it. Cut a lemon into fairly thick slices and tie them to the base of the artichoke with a length of twine to prevent discoloration while cooking. Cook the artichoke in a large pan of water containing salt, a little lemon juice and a dash of vinegar. It is ready when the leaves can be easily pulled out.

Artichoke Bottom for use as a Base

Using a sharp knife or one with a grooved blade, cut off the top of the artichoke to within about 4 or 5 cm (1½ to 2 in) of the base. Carefully remove the "choke" with a spoon and strip off all the leaves excepting the two or three innermost rows. A delicious artichoke bottom with rows of leaves remains.

Artichoke Bowl for Stuffing

Working from the centre of the artichoke, pull out the leaves until about two tall rows remain. Carefully remove the "choke" with a spoon, leaving a bowl for stuffing.

Breaking off the stalk

Straightening the base

Preparing for cooking

Removing the choke

Artichoke bowl for stuffing

Artichoke bottom with salad of prawns, carrots, mange-tout, quail's egg, olives and broccoli; right, artichoke bottom with asparagus and ham salad on a star of leaves. Centre, artichoke bottom with boletus mushrooms and tomato leaves. Below, left, artichoke bottom with sliced Spanish onion, mushrooms and chives; right, artichoke bowl with turned carrots and celeriac, courgettes (Zucchini (U.S.)), broccoli and tomato leaves.

GOURDS AND CUCUMBER

PUMPKIN, SQUASH AND MARROW

These all belong to the gourd family which includes a large number of different varieties. Apart from the vegetable marrow and the common orange-coloured pumpkin, there are the snake and the turban squash and also the vegetable spaghetti squash. The varieties differ in size, shape and colour, but they have one feature in common – their watery flesh has relatively little taste. The flesh of a ripe pumpkin or squash should be bright orange in

colour, firm and juicy, not soft or stringy. It should echo when the outside is gently tapped. Storage until the winter months presents no problems as long as a cool, airy place is available.

To prepare a pumpkin, cut it into segments from the stalk to the blossom end with a large, sharp knife and scoop out the soft, fibrous centre and the seeds with a spoon. Peel the segments before use. If the pumpkin skin is required intact, the flesh can be removed with a sharp-edged spoon.

COURGETTES (ZUCCHINI (U.S.))

Courgettes are a variety of small vegetable marrow with six sides. They are harvested while slightly unripe, when the skin is still soft; it may be pale or dark green in colour. Their average length is about 15 cm (6 in) and they weigh between 125 and 300 g ($4\frac{1}{2}$ and 10 oz). At this stage the flesh is light green and firm; a few seeds are embedded in it in the centre. When buying courgettes, care should be taken to reject the larger ones, which often have a yellowish

skin, a spongy texture and very little taste. Those which look wrinkled and wilted should also be avoided. Fresh courgettes will keep for up to a week without any difficulty in the vegetable crisper of the refrigerator.

N.B. Courgettes are not peeled before use as they would otherwise tend to break up while cooking. They are prepared by cutting off the stalk end and any brown spots which may be present.

Cucumber

The cucumber has been cultivated since early times. It probably originated in India. The different varieties range from the small, furrowed ones used for pickling to the long, smooth-skinned ones used as a salad vegetable. Cucumbers are available throughout the year, but the supply is most plentiful in the summer. Their quality depends, not on size, but on their consistency. A cucumber of the finest quality has quite firm flesh. Garnishes may be made with fresh cucumber and also with bottled pickled gherkins (Dill pickles (U.S.)).

Tools

The olive shaped and round Parisian cutters are used for cucumber and courgette decorations. The grooving knife and the fancy knife are required for cutting cucumber decoratively. The large one is used to cut up pumpkins and cucumber.

GOURDS AND CUCUMBER

PUMPKINS FOR STUFFING

Cut a slice off the pumpkin at the stalk end to make a lid, either by running the knife straight across or by cutting round the pumpkin zigzag fashion. Remove the seeds. Stuff the pumpkin and replace the lid on the slant to give access to the filling.

Pumpkin coronet

Pumpkin coronet with exotic fruit salad (about 50 portions)

GOURDS AND CUCUMBER

COURGETTE BOATS

Cut a courgette cylinder about 4 cm (1½ in) long, then cut this into quarters. Trim each one with a knife to the shape of a boat.

COURGETTE BASES

Cut small courgettes in half lengthwise and trim the underside of each half level for greater stability.

COURGETTE BARGES

Split large courgettes lengthwise and cut the halves into 7 cm (3 in) lengths, then round the ends off a little with a knife. Trim the undersides level for greater stability and hollow the halves out a little with a teaspoon.

COURGETTE TURRETS

Cut thick courgettes into about 4 cm (1½ in) lengths and hollow them out a little with a Parisian cutter. Taper the lower edge a little.

DECORATIONS WITH PICKLED GHERKINS (DILL PICKLES (U.S.))

SLICES

Drain the pickled gherkins well and cut into round, oval or lengthwise slices. Arrange in a ring, fan or row.

FAN

Make several incisions in the gherkin lengthwise, but do not cut right through to the end. Press the slices apart with the side of a knife to form a fan.

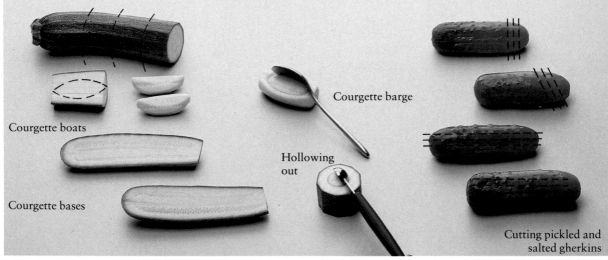

Courgette boats

Courgette bases

Courgette barge

Hollowing out

Cutting pickled and salted gherkins

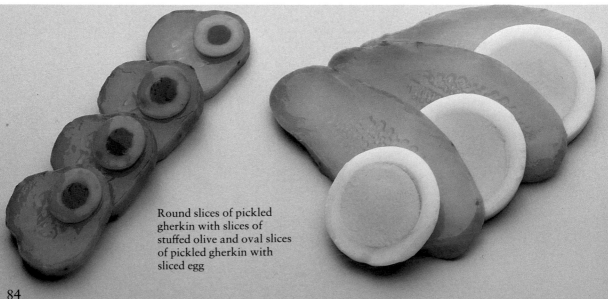

Round slices of pickled gherkin with slices of stuffed olive and oval slices of pickled gherkin with sliced egg

Half courgette with asparagus; right, courgette turret with mushroom and tomato salad. Centre, left, courgette barge with vegetable salad; right, decorative arrangement of courgette boats with a cherry tomato. Below, left, courgette boat on tomato; right, pickled gherkin fan on slice of egg

GOURDS AND CUCUMBER

DECORATIONS WITH FRESH CUCUMBER

SLICES

Groove the cucumber, cut it in slices and arrange these in a row.

HALF SLICES

Cut grooved cucumber slices in half and arrange in a row as an edging, slightly overlapping them.

WEDGES

Peel the cucumber, cut it in half lengthwise, then cut into wedges. Arrange these one behind another, side by side or in a ring.

BALLS OR OLIVES

Cut out balls or "olives" with a Parisian cutter, first peeling the cucumber if desired. Arrange the balls in a ring or assemble them into a bunch of "grapes". Cut the peel to the shape of leaves. Use the cucumber "olives" as a filling for cucumber boats or tomatoes.

CORONET

Cut an unpeeled cucumber into about 8 to 10 cm (3½ to 4 in) lengths. Cut each of these in half zigzag fashion and gently twist the halves apart.

Grooving

Grooved slices

Wedges

Cutting balls

Coronet

Cucumber wedges, a row of grooved
half cucumber slices; right, bunch of
cucumber grapes

Left, grooved cucumber slices
with tomato cut-outs; below,
cucumber coronet with turned
mushroom cap; right, stylised
cucumber flowers with sliced
egg and olive

Gourds and Cucumber

Cucumber for Stuffing

Cucumber Turrets

Cut the cucumber across into about 4 cm (1½ in) lengths and hollow these out with a Parisian cutter.

Cucumber Boats

Cut the cucumber in half lengthwise, then into 5 or 6 cm (about 2 in) lengths. Hollow these out a little with a teaspoon or Parisian cutter. Level off the base for greater stability.

Whole Cucumber

Select a choice cucumber of medium size. Wash it but leave unpeeled. Using a knife or peeler, cut a broad strip of peel from the blossom towards the stalk end, but do not cut it right off. Level off the underside of the cucumber a little for greater stability. Cut a thick grooved slice off a second cucumber for use on the ornamental skewer. Tie the strip of peel into a bow, wrapping the end round the outside of the thick cucumber slice. Insert the skewer into the end of the bow and push it right through into the stalk end of the cucumber. Using a teaspoon, hollow out the cucumber a little from end to end, then fill with a colourful mixed vegetable salad.

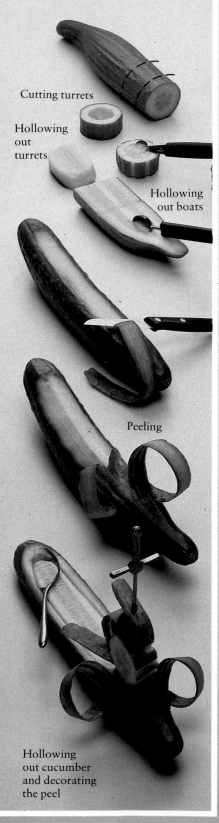

Cutting turrets

Hollowing out turrets

Hollowing out boats

Peeling

Hollowing out cucumber and decorating the peel

Grooved cucumber turret with cherry tomato and quarter quail's egg; below, cucumber turret with salad of celeriac and carrot olives; right, cucumber boat with slice of mushroom, cauliflower, broccoli, tomato leaves and half quail's egg; below, grooved cucumber turret with mushroom salad

Cucumber stuffed with
mixed vegetable salad

MUSHROOMS

Medium-size white mushrooms with closed caps should be selected for garnishing. Wash them well and sprinkle with a little lemon juice to keep them white for some time. If older mushrooms with darkish woody stalks are used, the stalks should be cut back to firm flesh.

MUSHROOM SLICES

After washing, cut the mushrooms into slices and arrange these one behind another.

There are brown and white varieties. They taste best when freshly prepared. They may, however, be stored in the vegetable compartment of the refrigerator, where they will keep for about three or four days. They should never be stored in plastic bags.

WHAT TO LOOK FOR WHEN BUYING MUSHROOMS

Mushrooms are sold both trimmed and untrimmed. The former are smaller and include button mushrooms; they have tight caps and trimmed stalks. They only require washing under running water and are then left to drain on kitchen paper.

When dry, the stalks may be trimmed further if desired. The untrimmed ones are generally fresher and have more flavour. They should also be washed under running water, then thoroughly dried. The stalks are shortened a little before use.

TOOLS

The vegetable knife is used together with the grooving knife to cut and decorate mushrooms.

Mushroom slices with tomato and sweet pepper cut-outs; grooved mushroom cap stuffed with chestnut, prune, silver-skin onions and pistachios; centre, grooved mushroom cap on a cut-out cucumber star; turned mushroom cap; slice of mushroom with carrot and cucumber balls; right, stuffed mushroom caps with vegetable balls on a cut-out slice of sweet pepper and with small tomato salad

GROOVED MUSHROOM CAP

Starting from the centre of the cap, draw the grooving knife downwards six or eight times all round. Sprinkle with lemon juice.

TURNED MUSHROOM CAP

Working with the blade of a sharp knife held at a slight angle between the thumb and forefinger, draw the knife downwards from the centre of the cap repeatedly sickle fashion. Sprinkle the cap with lemon juice.

Grooving

Turning

Preparing the cap for stuffing

STUFFED MUSHROOM CAPS

For this decoration, mushrooms of the same size should be used. Wash them and cut off the stalks. If necessary, hollow out a little with a Parisian cutter before stuffing. Once the stuffing is in place and firmly pressed into the hollow, the mushroom cap may be floured and shallow fried in butter. Salt and pepper are added during frying. Alternatively, the stuffed mushroom cap may be seasoned with salt and pepper, floured, egg and crumbed, then deep fried. (A suitable stuffing for both these versions is given in the recipe section.)

BREAD AND ROLLS

FLAT BREAD BASKET

To present a combination of various types of sliced bread a flat basket is used. A broad ribbon is tied round it with a bow and it is lined inside with a napkin matching the colour of the tablecloth. A variety of breads should be selected, including brown, wholemeal, rye, mixed grain and rolls of various kinds as well as French sticks.

TALL BREAD BASKET

A cold buffet is obviously accompanied by bread and rolls, which may be very attractively displayed. If a combination of rolls, croissants, pretzels, French breads and savoury sticks is selected, a tall basket should be used, preferably one with a handle. A broad ribbon is wound round the handle and one end is tied in a fairly large bow. The other side of the handle may be decorated by tying on a bunch of wheat-ears or alternatively a pretzel or croissant.

92

Choux Pastry Goods

Basic Recipe

The ingredients required for choux pastry are: $\frac{1}{4}$ l ($\frac{1}{2}$ pt approx.) water; 50 g (2 oz) butter; pinch of salt; 150 g (5 oz) flour; 2 eggs; fat for baking off.

Place the water, butter and salt in a pan and heat until the water boils. Add the flour and stir until the mixture forms into a ball, leaving the sides of the pan clean. Transfer to a bowl and beat in the eggs one at a time. The paste is of the right consistency when it drops quickly from the spoon in peaks.

Choux Paste Shapes

By means of a savoy bag fitted with different tubes (star or plain) choux paste may be piped out to make decorative garnishes such as finger shapes for éclairs, "S" shapes for madelons, small bulbs for rosettes, two smaller bulbs side by side for double rosettes, and semicircles for crescents.

Swans

To make a swan the choux paste is piped in two separate parts. The head and neck are made first, starting with the beak, which is thinner than the rest and angled upwards to a length of about 1 cm ($\frac{1}{2}$ in). For the head the bag is squeezed a little harder, then the neck is piped evenly in the form of an "S". A bulb or oblong is piped out for the body.

Choux pastries with savoury fillings (see recipe section): above, éclairs and swan; centre, single and double rosettes; below, crescent and madelons

95

Butter Garnishes

Butter

Butter is a natural dairy product obtained from cream which has been skimmed off milk. It can be made from fresh or sour cream. It is sometimes salted to improve its keeping qualities.

Tools

Various tools may be used to prepare butter garnishes. The special butter cutter combines several functions. It will produce butter balls, fluted slices or curls. The ribbed butter shapers ("Scotch hands") are used for moulding balls.

Butter moulds consist of two parts, the barrel and the rammer. A relief design is carved into the end of the rammer. It can be used to decorate pats of butter with attractive patterns in relief. Butter cut into slices about $\frac{1}{2}$ cm ($\frac{1}{4}$ in) thick may be neatly trimmed with a variety of small cutters.

Sliced Butter Garnishes

Dip the central portion of the butter cutter into boiling hot water and use it to cut a slice off the butter. Both sides will be fluted.

Cut-out Butter Garnishes

Cut the butter into slices and shape with small cutters of suitable size, then place the cut-outs in iced water.

Cut-out butter

Sliced butter; right, decorative butter
wedges with tomato rose and radish
rose

Butter Garnishes

Butter Balls

Dip the butter cutter into boiling hot water, press it on to the butter, which should not be too hard, and turn it smoothly while pressing. Place the balls in a bowl of cold water containing ice cubes. For various decorations butter balls may be moulded between two ribbed butter shapers. They may also be rolled in red paprika or finely chopped herbs.

Butter Grapes

About 30 to 40 butter balls are required for a bunch of grapes. To make the stalk and leaves, cut slices of butter with a knife dipped in hot water, then cut out with the aid of stencils and arrange on a plate. Vein the leaves with the back of a knife. Add plain or fluted butter balls assembled into a bunch.

Moulded Butter Reliefs

Butter trimmings may be used for spreading or shaped in a butter mould.
Place the mould in cold water for a few minutes before use. Soften the butter, press it into the mould, then push down the rammer to force out a butter pat stamped with a design in relief.

Butter Curls

The butter cutter may be used to make curls. Stand a 250 g (9 oz) pack of butter on its side and smoothly draw the cutter along the upper long side from end to end. Place the curls in iced water.

Butter Rose

Cream the butter which has been brought to room temperature and fill into a savoy bag with a petal pipe. Insert the eye end of a 10 cm (4 in) darning needle into a cork and the point into a firm half apple. Wrap the top of the cork in aluminium foil. Now pipe the butter on to the cork while rotating the latter carefully until a small bud has been fashioned. Pipe on small inside petals about 3 or 4 cm (1½ in) wide while gently swinging the pipe upwards. The outside petals should be made a little wider and longer. Carefully blow down on to the rose to open it out a little. Place it in the refrigerator on its base to harden.

Butter balls

Paprika and herb coated balls

Butter mould

Butter curls

Butter rose

Butter grapes, butter roses, butter
curls and individual pats shaped in
the butter mould; below, right,
paprika and herb coated butter balls

EGG GARNISHES

HENS' EGGS

Eggs are graded according to size from the largest (size 1) weighing 70 g (2½ oz) and over down to the smallest (size 6) weighing less than 40 g (1½ oz). They vary, not only in size, weight and colour, but also in freshness.

When used for garnishing, hens' eggs should be boiled for about 10 minutes, then plunged at once into cold water to facilitate shelling.

QUAILS' AND GULLS' EGGS

Quails' eggs should be boiled for about 5 minutes, gulls' eggs for about 8 minutes. They should not be shelled completely; about one third of the shell is removed from the small end only.

BOILING EGGS

Eggs should be pricked before boiling; a special implement may be bought for this purpose. A very small hole is made in the larger, rounded end of the egg where the air chamber is situated. This method applies to all eggs, including quails' and gulls' eggs (in season early June).

Testing Eggs for Freshness

The freshness of an egg may be tested by immersion in a tumbler of water. A fresh egg has very little air inside the shell and is relatively heavy. Consequently it will sink to the bottom of the glass and remain resting there. A one-week old egg, on the other hand, has an increased amount of air inside its rounded end, which will rise at an angle to the bottom of the glass. If the egg is two to three weeks old it contains even more air, which makes it buoyant enough for the rounded end to be raised to a vertical position. Once it is five or six weeks old, an egg will float on the surface; it should not be used.

Tools

The two different types of egg cutters provide a quick method of cutting up eggs. The fancy knife is used for egg white decorations. Stuffed eggs may be attractively prepared by filling them with the aid of a savoy bag fitted with a star tube.

The special tool with a needle makes it easy to prick the shell before boiling an egg to prevent it from cracking.

101

Egg Garnishes

Egg Slices and Segments

Two different types of cutters are used for hard-boiled hens' eggs. They produce either even slices or six segments. The slicer may be used to cut strips or dice by turning the egg round after slicing. These are suitable garnishes for green salads.

Egg Halves

There are two ways of cutting a hard-boiled egg in half, lengthwise or crosswise. In either case the base should be trimmed flat for greater stability.

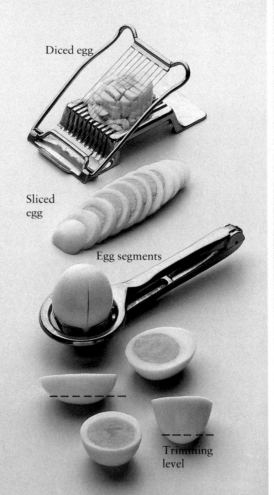

Diced egg

Sliced egg

Egg segments

Trimming level

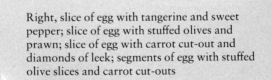

Right, slice of egg with tangerine and sweet pepper; slice of egg with stuffed olives and prawn; slice of egg with carrot cut-out and diamonds of leek; segments of egg with stuffed olive slices and carrot cut-outs

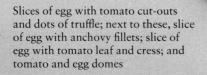

Slices of egg with tomato cut-outs and dots of truffle; next to these, slice of egg with anchovy fillets; slice of egg with tomato leaf and cress; and tomato and egg domes

Chopped egg on grooved cucumber slices with strips of radish, and egg halves with salami cone, rolled-up Bündnerfleisch, and asparagus

Egg and tomato segments with stuffed olive slices

EGG GARNISHES

LILY OF THE VALLEY

Slice a hard-boiled egg evenly with the slicer and remove the yolk, which may be used in salads or sandwiches. Stamp out rounds of egg white with a plain piping tube and cut off a third of each, using a fancy knife with a serrated edge, to make stylised small bell-like flowers. Cut stems and leaves of braised leek with a sharp knife and assemble to a spray of lily of the valley with the white flowers.

EGG YOLK PASTE

For two hard-boiled eggs 20 g ($\frac{3}{4}$ oz) butter is required, with a little salt, pepper and mustard.

Shell the eggs and carefully cut in half lengthwise with a knife. Using a tablespoon, rub the yolks through a fine sieve into a bowl. Soften the butter and mix with the yolks, salt, pepper and mustard to taste, creaming the mixture well.

N.B. Should the paste become too stiff, stand the bowl over a pan of warm water and beat to the desired consistency. Should the paste be too soft, almost beginning to liquefy, place it in the refrigerator and mix well from time to time. Trim the underside of the egg-white cups a little for greater stability, then place them in a bowl of salted water. Pipe the filling into the whites through a star tube and garnish.

Egg slices

Egg halves

Cut-out and trimmed egg white flower

Stuffed eggs

Quails' eggs on a nest of cress and radishes; below, left, stuffed eggs with various garnishes; below, right, lily of the valley

Sweet and Savoury Aspic Glazes

Jelly Glaze for Fruit

10 leaves gelatine (best quality) in warm weather or 8 leaves gelatine in cold weather; $\frac{1}{2}$ l (approx. 1 pt) dry white wine; juice of $\frac{1}{4}$ lemon; 70 g (2$\frac{1}{2}$ oz) sugar.

Soak the gelatine in cold water for about 10 minutes, then squeeze out well. Bring the wine almost to the boil in a small pan, then remove from the heat. Add the gelatine and stir slowly until dissolved. Now add the lemon juice and sugar and stir until almost cool enough to set (the jelly will set at about 28–30°C (85°F)). Apply the jelly to the fruit with a pastry brush.

Madeira Aspic for Meat Dishes

450 g (1 lb) clear oxtail soup; 50 g (2 oz) Madeira; pinch of salt; 20 g ($\frac{3}{4}$ oz) aspic powder (for medium soft jelly); or 40–50 g (1$\frac{1}{2}$–2 oz) aspic powder (for very firm jelly).

Strain the oxtail soup through a cloth to remove any fat or meat. Soak the aspic powder for about 10 minutes in a third of the strained cold soup. Bring the rest of the soup to the boil, add the aspic, stir slowly until dissolved, then stir in the Madeira. Transfer to a flat dish and place in the refrigerator to set.

Dill Aspic for Fish Dishes

500 g (1 lb 2 oz) clear fish stock (made with dry white wine); 20 g ($\frac{3}{4}$ oz) aspic powder (for medium soft jelly); or 40–50 g (1$\frac{1}{2}$–2 oz) aspic powder (for very firm jelly); 1 bunch dill.

Soak the aspic powder for about 10 minutes in about a third of the cold fish stock. Bring the rest of the stock to the boil, add the aspic and stir slowly until dissolved. Cut the dill very finely. Stir the fish aspic over a pan of cold water until almost setting (it will set at about 35°C (95°F)) before adding the dill.

<u>N.B.</u> If the dill is added just before the jelly sets it will not sink to the bottom.

WORKING WITH ASPIC

Aspic powder is a type of gelatine which is added to stock or broth to make savoury jelly. It is a pure protein substance; consequently, all the tools and utensils, such as whisks, bowls and pans, must be especially clean, for an aspic solution is a particularly good medium for the growth of micro-organisms.

REMOVING FAT

If aspic is prepared with beef or chicken stock, globules of fat may form. While the jelly is warm these are transparent, but when it sets they become cold and hard, collecting on the surface in small or large patches. To avoid this, an absorbent paper napkin is placed on the surface of the liquid before it cools, then lifted off, removing the globules of fat. If any remain, the process should be repeated.

Cutting out aspic shapes

TOOLS

A ruler and a knife are used to cut blocks of aspic into various shapes. Fancy cutters of various kinds are used to cut out aspic decorations. A brush is useful for glazing meat dishes or vegetable decorations with aspic. Aspic trimmings are coarsely chopped with a knife, providing a quick decorative edging for a dish.

Chopped aspic

Sweet and Savoury Aspic Glazes

Aspic Coating for Meat and Fish

1. Cool the aspic to about 34°C (93°F) and apply to the meat or fish with a soft brush.
2. Place the meat or fish to be glazed on a pastry rack and pour the aspic over with a ladle. The excess will drain away, but a thin coating will remain.

Lining Serving Dishes with Aspic

To find out how much aspic is needed, water is first poured into the dish to the desired level, then transferred to a clean pan. For lining a dish the aspic should be particularly firm. For 1 l (1¾ pt) water 70 g (2½ oz) aspic powder should be used. It is dissolved as already described, then run over the bottom of the dish to the depth of about 5 mm (¼ in). If any bubbles form, they may be removed by tapping gently with the finger or the flat side of a knife.

Coating sliced meat with aspic

Brushing aspic on to a slice of ham

Dipping melon balls in aspic

Lining a dish with aspic

If the dish is not standing level and the aspic collects at one end, a knife may be placed underneath to level the dish. It should not be touched again until the aspic has set. When the jelly is firm enough no ripples will form on the surface if air is blown on to it. The meat or fish may be placed on top once the aspic has set firmly.

Dish lined with aspic and decorated with aspic jelly shapes cut with a knife or cutters. It contains sliced roast beef, asparagus, ham, sliced egg, radishes and gherkins

109

Sweet and Savoury Aspic Glazes

Flowers Under Aspic

Whites of 3 eggs; 2 slices hard-boiled egg yolk; 16 small ovals of black garnishing paste or truffle; 2 leaves and stems cut from braised leek or cucumber peel.

Place the whites in a buttered cup and cook over a pan of hot water at 80°C (175°F) until set and firm. Cut out two rounds of hard-boiled egg yolk with a plain 1½ to 2 cm (¾ in) cutter. Slice the whites thinly, then cut with an oval cutter. Sixteen ovals are required. Place a black oval on each white one, first dipping them in aspic. Brush the yolk cut-outs all round with aspic to prevent particles crumbling off later and spoiling the aspic coating. Allow the yolk cut-outs to dry, then dip in aspic again and place on the dish. Arrange the white ovals round them, first dipping them in aspic again. Lastly add the leaves and stems. Refrigerate to set the aspic. Meanwhile cool the aspic jelly required to line the dish to about 36–38°C (97–100°F), then run it on to the bottom of the dish. N.B. The jelly for lining the dish has to be very cool so that the garnish which has been fixed in place with jelly does not come away and float to the surface.

Cutting out egg whites

Cutting out garnishing paste

Brushing with aspic

Cutting out egg yolk

Cutting leek

Dish with flowers under aspic and stuffed ham rolls

COCKTAIL TITBITS AND CANAPÉS

COCKTAIL TITBITS

These are made with plain or fluted cut-out rounds of pumpernickel, white, brown or rye bread. The topping, which may be sausage, cheese, fish, fruit or vegetables, is secured by means of a cocktail stick. The bases are cut out with 34 to 36 mm (about 1¼ in) pastry cutters.

garnished with a wide variety of toppings. For canapés, which are more elegant in appearance than cocktail titbits, the use of cocktail sticks is inappropriate. Canapés may be made in various shapes:— 5½ to 6 cm (2½ in) rounds, 6½ × 4 cm (2½ × 1½ in) ovals, 6 × 4 cm (2½ × 1½ in) rectangles, or 7 cm (3 in) triangles.

CANAPÉS

The canapés described here are small toasted or plain slices of white tin or sandwich loaf. They are buttered and

TOOLS

Pastry cutters, knives and cocktail sticks are required for the preparation of the various titbits and canapés.

Folded slice of smoked ham fillet with asparagus and stuffed olive slices

Crème des Prés cheese with pepper cheese and cress

Parma style ham with half slice of egg and gherkin fan

Slices of egg with anchovy fillets and capers

Roast beef with sliced palm hearts and hot dog relish

Lettuce, sliced pickled gherkin, matjes herring fillet, slice of egg and sliced onion

Left, titbit with cut-out rounds of Gouda and pear, Roquefort cream, almond and cocktail cherry; right, smoked ham fillet stuffed with asparagus on round of Tilsit cheese, decorated with a melon ball; below, rolled matjes herring strip on egg yolk cut-out, decorated with a silverskin onion

Smoked salmon with cut-out half slice of egg, horseradish cream, scampi and capers

Gouda cheese, rolled slice of roast beef stuffed with horseradish cream and gherkin

Slice of Appenzell cheese, Gouda cube, tomato leaf with silverskin onion

Cheshire cheese, salami cone, sliced gherkin and silverskin onion

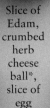

Slice of cucumber, ball of steak tartare*, anchovy fillet, olive

Slice of Edam, crumbed herb cheese ball*, slice of egg

Slice of Emmental cheese, Bündnerfleisch stuffed with white cheese cream, olive

(*See recipe section)

113

COCKTAIL TITBITS AND CANAPÉS

PRESENTATION

STRAIGHT LINE ARRANGEMENT

The titbits or canapés are placed directly next to and behind one another to form straight lines. This type of presentation is recommended for large serving dishes, but the size of the dish should be in keeping with the number of titbits or canapés, to avoid any large gaps.

"STAGGERED" ARRANGEMENT

This type of presentation is recommended where as many titbits and canapés as possible have to be served on a fairly small dish. In this case the canapés are arranged in straight lines, while the titbits are fitted between the horizontal lines in a staggered pattern. This has the advantage of offering a wide choice for the palate and a variety of colours for the eye.

"V" SHAPED ARRANGEMENT

For a round dish presentation the way in which the canapés and titbits are arranged depends on the number of items to be included. If the number is fairly small, a straight line arrangement is used, but for a large number a "V" arrangement is best.

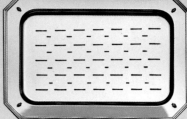

"Staggered" arrangement

Straight line arrangement on rectangular and oval dish

"V" shaped arrangement

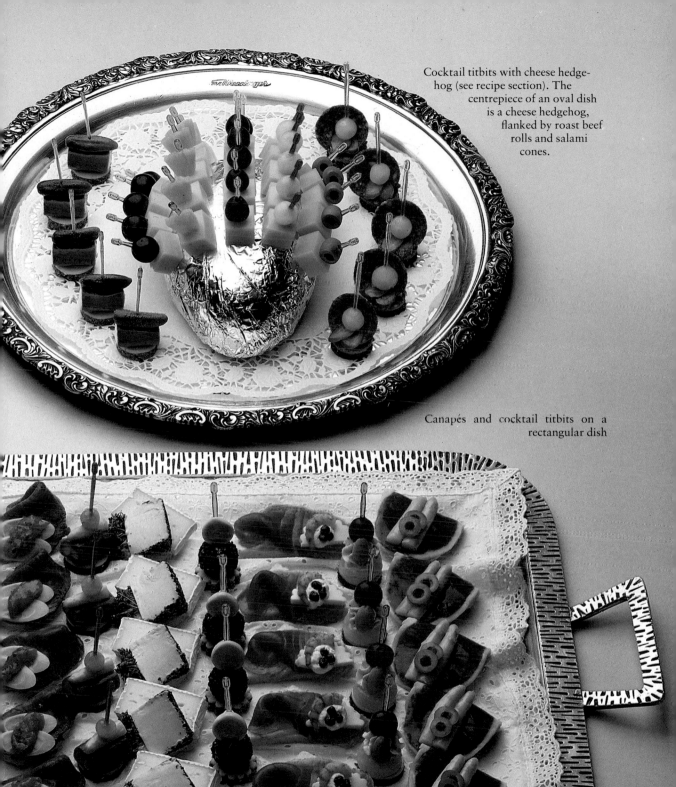

Cocktail titbits with cheese hedgehog (see recipe section). The
centrepiece of an oval dish
is a cheese hedgehog,
flanked by roast beef
rolls and salami
cones.

Canapés and cocktail titbits on a
rectangular dish

Medallions and Cocktails

Medallions

These are small delicacies which may be used for hors d'oeuvre, cold dishes and buffets. They are made from fillet of beef, veal or pork and garnished with vegetables and savoury butters or creams. Seafood medallions can also be made to look very attractive and go particularly well with fresh vegetables, especially cucumber or freshly prepared artichoke bottoms.

Cocktails

Many different types of special cocktail glasses are on sale, including some with a cobalt blue or gold rim or others of ornamented cut glass. Even a perfectly plain glass may be given a decorative rim by means of sugar frosting, perhaps with the addition of different food colours to provide variety.

Ingredients for scampi fan on an artichoke bottom

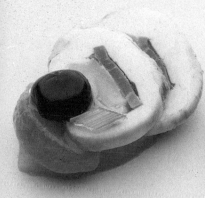

Stuffed breast of chicken (from delicatessen store) with mandarin segments, cocktail cherry and lozenge of angelica on pineapple

Asparagus with strips of Bündnerfleisch on cucumber, slice of egg and ham butter (see recipe section)

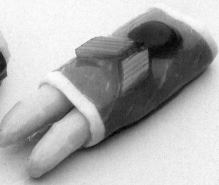

Smoked ham fillet stuffed with asparagus, decorated with cocktail cherries and lozenges of angelica

Pork medallion with meat glaze (see recipe section), chicken liver paste (see recipe section), preserved ginger and walnut

Fillet of veal with meat glaze (see recipe section), chicken liver paste (see recipe section), almond and melon ball

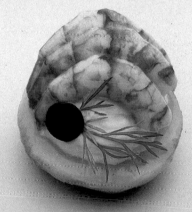

Artichoke bottom, horseradish cream (see recipe section), scampi fan, sprig of dill and truffle disc

Smoked eel with dill and slices of olive on cucumber, slice of egg and horseradish cream (see recipe section)

Rolled matjes herring with half quail's egg and tomato disc on cucumber and slice of egg

Anchovy trio with sliced olive and silverskin onion on cucumber and slice of egg

117

MEDALLIONS AND COCKTAILS

PRESENTATION

SYMMETRICAL ARRANGEMENT

The medallions are arranged symmetrically to the right and left of the centrepiece.

Symmetrical arrangement

Asymmetrical arrangement

Herring-bone arrangement

HERRING-BONE ARRANGEMENT

The medallions are arranged in a herring-bone pattern. <u>N.B.</u> The medallions may be easily arranged in a line with the help of two knives tied together by a long piece of twine. The twine is held taut by sliding the knives underneath the dish at opposite ends.

ASYMMETRICAL ARRANGEMENT

The main eye-catching feature is placed in one corner of the dish. A suitable example might be an arrangement of vegetables in sweet pepper halves, decorated with cucumber wedges. The medallions are arranged asymmetrically to cover the rest of the dish.

Dish with "V" shaped arrangement of
medallions. The eye-catching feature
is a vegetable salad in sweet
pepper halves with
wedges of cucumber.

119

MEDALLIONS AND COCKTAILS

SUGAR FROSTING FOR RIM

Place a little egg white or melted aspic jelly on a plate. Mix a little sugar with a drop of food colour and spread evenly on a second plate. Dip the top of the cocktail glass to a depth of about 2 mm ($\frac{1}{12}$ in) into the egg white or aspic, then into the sugar. Remove and tap off the excess.

<u>N.B.</u> Red sugar frosting looks particularly attractive with pale cocktails; white is very suitable for dark ones. For mixed lettuce, vegetable, game and fish cocktails the rim of the glass may be decorated with herbs. These are very finely chopped and dried by squeezing in a kitchen cloth. As described above, the rim of the glass is dipped first in egg white or aspic, then in the dry herbs.

Red sugar frosted glass rim

Above, scampi cocktail (see recipe section)

Left, marinated lobster on lettuce (see recipe section)

Above, left, asparagus cocktail (see recipe section); above, right, Dublin Bay prawn (scampi) cocktail (see recipe section); left, King prawns in melon (see recipe section)

121

NAPKINS AND PAPER FRILLS

NAPKIN DECORATION FOR DEEP DISH

ARTICHOKE

A starched napkin is used. The four corners are first folded towards the middle. The resulting new corners are again folded towards the middle. Now the napkin is turned over and the four corners are again folded towards the middle. The outside edges should be firmly pressed together with the hand. The centre of the napkin is now grasped in one hand while the points that have formed on the other side are opened up. Once all four of them are in position the corners that were lying in between may be pulled out sideways.

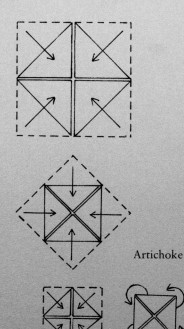

Artichoke

NAPKIN DECORATION FOR FLAT DISH

GONDOLA

A well starched napkin is used. For large dishes it is best to use a large, strong napkin, reinforced by lining it with aluminium foil. The two top corners are first brought towards the middle and the edges are pressed down to make a smooth fold. The resulting new corners are again brought towards the middle and the edges are firmly pressed down. Then the corners are folded inwards again. The napkin is now folded down the middle, the two halves being placed exactly one on top of the other.

The napkin is now placed in the centre of a towel, which is folded over it; the folded ends should be pointing towards the body. The towel is laid on the edge of the table and weighted with a board. While the board is firmly held down with the left (or right) hand, the towel is jerked towards the body, making very fine pleats in the napkin.

The shape of the gondola is adjusted a little by hand, then it is two thirds opened out and the top is shaped to form a coiled rosette.

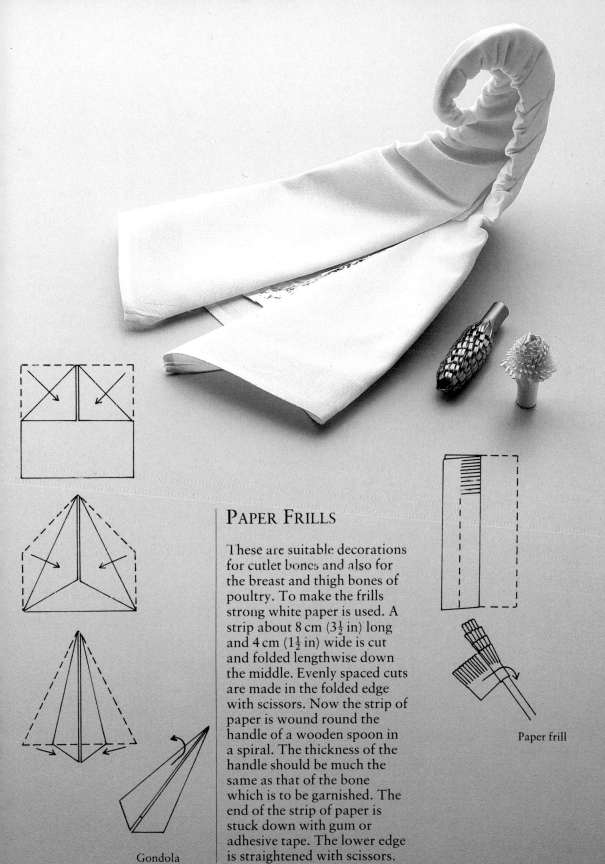

PAPER FRILLS

These are suitable decorations for cutlet bones and also for the breast and thigh bones of poultry. To make the frills strong white paper is used. A strip about 8 cm (3½ in) long and 4 cm (1½ in) wide is cut and folded lengthwise down the middle. Evenly spaced cuts are made in the folded edge with scissors. Now the strip of paper is wound round the handle of a wooden spoon in a spiral. The thickness of the handle should be much the same as that of the bone which is to be garnished. The end of the strip of paper is stuck down with gum or adhesive tape. The lower edge is straightened with scissors.

Gondola

Paper frill

Sweet Decorations

Moulded and Piped Decoration

Decorated heart for Mother's Day coated with buttercream and decorated with buttercream pearls. The roses are modelled with coloured marzipan. The marzipan scroll is inscribed with a message in chocolate icing. The petits fours, to be enjoyed at any time, are coated with white icing and decorated with piped filigree ornaments.

FRUIT AND CONFECTIONERY DESSERTS

A favourite dessert for children is a pear hedgehog with chocolate sauce on mangoes, while adults enjoy banana split decorated with mixed fruit and a topping of whipped cream. At the end of the meal coffee is served with biscuits decorated with coloured icing and candied fruit, petits fours decorated with marzipan figures and icing, or an exotic fruit tart or gâteau with rings of ruit and a piped edging of whipped dairy cream.

SWEET DECORATIONS

FRUIT AND CREAM

In hot summer weather it is refreshing to eat a fruit tartlet decorated with whipped cream or a pastry motif, or perhaps a vanilla bombe with buttercream pearls and chocolate ornaments. Whipped cream toppings with sugar strands and fresh strawberries are also enjoyed, as are iced "moors' heads" with funny faces.

SWEET DECORATIONS

SPECIAL OCCASIONS

For special festive occasions and large gatherings more elaborate and costly decoration is called for. The three tier wedding cake is coated with delicate buttercream and decorated with numerous white pearls of buttercream. The top of each tier is edged with pink marzipan flowers each having a silver ball in the centre. The cherry dome gâteau is covered with whipped cream and fine chocolate flakes. The eye-catching feature consists of two cocktail cherries with stalks on a round of icing sugar.

The fine gâteau with the catkin motif is first coated with lemon icing. Depending on the time of year and the occasion, the gâteau may be decorated with willow twigs or other motifs taken from nature which are piped on in coloured icing.

BUTTERCREAM DECORATIONS

GERMAN BUTTERCREAM

$\frac{1}{2}$ l (approx. 1 pt) milk; 1 sachet vanilla custard powder; 50 g (2 oz) sugar; 2 egg yolks; 1 small glass orange liqueur; 350 g (12 oz) butter.
Place three quarters of the milk in a pan and bring to the boil. Blend the custard powder smoothly with the rest of the milk and add carefully to the boiling milk. Stir in the sugar and cook as directed on the sachet. Remove from the heat and allow to cool a little. Blend in the yolks and liqueur and leave until quite cold. Meanwhile cream the butter, brought to room temperature, until very soft and white, using a mixer, and add the custard.

FRENCH BUTTERCREAM

3 eggs; 4 egg yolks; 150 g (5 oz) sugar; 1 sachet vanilla sugar; 1 small glass orange liqueur; 350 g (12 oz) butter.
Place the eggs and yolks in a heatproof bowl, add the sugar and liqueur and whisk to a thick custard over heat. Remove from the heat and beat until cold. Meanwhile cream the butter in a mixer until very soft and white, then add the custard.

COLOURED BUTTERCREAM

Buttercream may be coloured and flavoured in many different ways, but it is essential for all the colouring and flavouring ingredients to be at room temperature or very finely ground before being mixed with the buttercream.
For dark brown buttercream, nougat paste, chocolate, or coffee flavoured with rum may be used. Strawberry or raspberry purée or finely ground nuts such as hazels or pistachios provide pretty colours and fine flavour.

Decorations
for gâteaux and
buttercream
slices piped with
plain or star tubes
as desired

TOOLS

For buttercream decorations a savoy bag is required with the following icing tubes as a minimum: star tubes size 5, 7 and 9, and plain tubes size 6, 8 and 10. Coarse tubes Nos. 9 and 10 are used specifically for dairy cream gâteaux.

CONTINUOUS EDGING

For edging a plain tube size 8 or a star tube size 7 is required.

DOTTED EDGING

Squeeze the buttercream out of the bag until the dot is of the desired size, then release the pressure and lift the tube away.

PEARL EDGING

Squeeze the buttercream out of the bag until the pearl is of the desired size, reduce the pressure and move the tube forwards to lift it off.

OFFSET PEARL EDGING

Proceed as for pearl edging, but alternately move the tube to the left and right to lift it off.

"CATERPILLAR" EDGING

Pipe out even-size rings extending forwards in a spiral.

HOW TO HOLD A SAVOY BAG

The lower end of the bag is held between the thumb and forefinger of the left (or right) hand and guided by the same hand. The other hand is used to hold the top of the bag securely and squeeze the buttercream out through the tube.

Buttercream Decorations

Decorations for Individual Torte Portions

Tubes size 6 and 8 may be used for these decorations.
Pipe out the centre finger first, then the two on either side.
Pipe out the longest finger first, then the two shorter ones, lastly the dot. Add chocolate leaves, walnuts or pistachios for final decoration.
Pipe out the two fingers first, then the dots between them.
Turn the portion of torte, pipe on a capital "L" and place an ornament on the loop. Pipe out a thin "S" shape. Place an ornament on the lower loop. A star tube may be used for this shape.
Pipe out two half "S" shapes one next to the other. An ornament may be placed over the point where they meet.
Pipe out a "Z" shape. An ornament may be placed in the larger of the two spaces.
N.B. Stiffly whipped dairy cream may be used for these decorations.

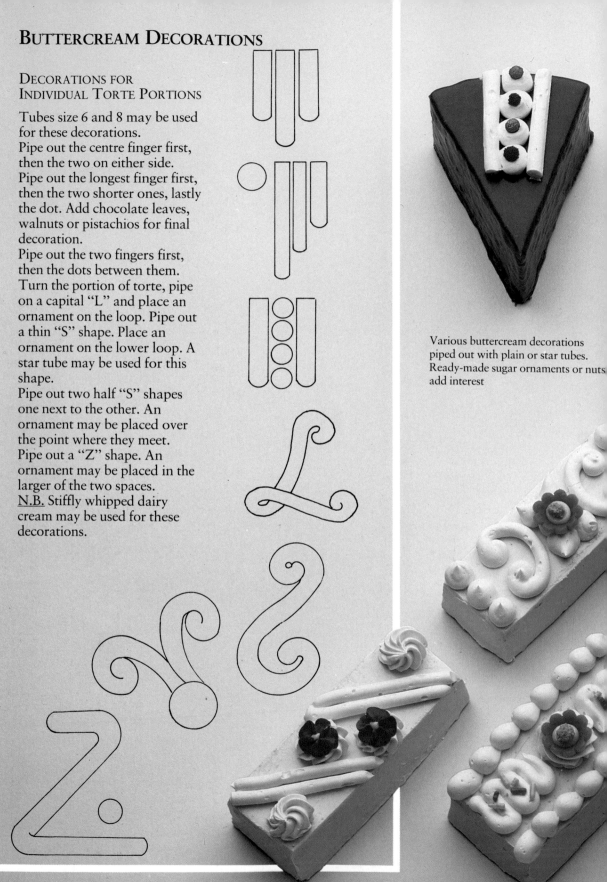

Various buttercream decorations piped out with plain or star tubes. Ready-made sugar ornaments or nuts add interest

CHOCOLATE AND OTHER ICINGS

CHOCOLATE ICING

For chocolate icing professional bakers mainly use couverture. When buying, take care not to purchase ordinary block chocolate, which contains too little fat and needs to be enriched with cocoa butter or coconut butter. Couverture may be plain or milk. Eating chocolate may also be used. It consists of cocoa-mass with the addition of sugar and some cocoa butter; sometimes milk, dairy cream or flavouring ingredients are also added.

TEMPERING

Place the couverture in a dry bowl and stand this on a pan containing warm water. Never place the bowl over direct heat as chocolate burns easily.
As soon as the couverture has melted completely, leave it in a cool place until just beginning to set. It is at this point that it has to be very carefully reheated. Stand the bowl on a pan of warm water again from time to time while stirring constantly until the couverture reaches a temperature of 32°C (90°F), the melting point of cocoa butter.

<u>N.B.</u> If couverture is heated beyond 34°C (93°F) the cocoa butter separates off and forms a fat bloom on the surface of the couverture, once it has cooled and set. This spoils the appearance, though it does not affect the quality.

KNIFE TEST

To be certain that the couverture has reached the correct melting point, dip the point of a knife into it and remove a little. Set the knife aside (preferably in the refrigerator) and allow the couverture on it to set. If it has done so after two or three minutes the temperature is right.

OTHER ICINGS

There are two main basic recipes for icings made with icing sugar. For royal icing, about 200 g (7 oz) icing sugar should be mixed with one egg white.

For water icing, 2 to 3 tablespoons boiling water are mixed with 200 g (7 oz) icing sugar. In both cases the icing is passed through a fine sieve to ensure that it is smooth and free from lumps. It is then covered with a damp cloth to prevent skinning.

<u>N.B.</u> Icings may be given different flavours and colours by the addition of suitable flavourings. Food colours may be used for increased effect.

TOOLS

A spatula, a knife and various small cutters are used to work with chocolate for decorations.

PIPING BAG FOR THIN LINES

Fold a rectangular piece of greaseproof paper diagonally and cut through the fold with a sharp knife. Hold the triangular piece of paper between the thumb, forefinger and second finger; using the thumb and forefinger of the other hand, fold the ends of the long edge inwards to shape the paper into a cone.

FILLING THE BAG WITH ICING

Insert the bag into the neck of a bottle to hold it steady while filling. The bag should not be more than just over half full of icing. Fold the pointed top of the bag towards the front, then fold the left and right sides inwards and roll the folded part over to form a pressure level.

Snip off the point of the bag with a pair of scissors according to the piping thickness desired. The further the cut is from the tip, the thicker the flow of icing will be.

CHOCOLATE AND OTHER ICINGS

The following pages demonstrate the versatility of chocolate and other icings for making ornaments. The procedure is quite simple and excellent results can be achieved with a steady hand.

DESIGN FOR INDIVIDUAL PORTION OF TORTE

The chocolate ornament below is very frequently used on festive torten. The icing is poured into a paper bag and

piped out in the shape of a wide, flat bow. A second bow, longer and wider than the first, is now piped on top. Lastly, the two bows are joined together by means of a tall peak.

PIPING CHOCOLATE ORNAMENTS (RUN-OUTS)

To make these remarkable little creations, the first requirement is a sheet of paper on which the desired pattern is drawn with a black felt-tipped pen. A sheet of greaseproof paper* is placed on top. The chocolate icing is poured into a paper bag. The outline showing through the greaseproof paper is then piped over and the ornaments are left to set hard before being removed with a sharp knife.
N.B. Only well tempered couverture should be used for piping chocolate ornaments. If the couverture runs too much while being piped out, a drop of water may be added, but

this should be done with care as water hardens it.

STORING CHOCOLATE ORNAMENTS

To avoid the trouble of piping ornaments every time they are required, a supply of them can be made in advance. The ornaments, piped on to greaseproof paper, are arranged in layers in a tin or plastic container with an airtight lid. The storage temperature should be 10–15°C (50–60°F) to ensure that the chocolate does not melt. It will keep for several weeks if stored under these conditions.
Alternatively, the ornaments may be frozen after arranging them in layers in a suitable container.
N.B. These chocolate ornaments are not only suitable for torten; they make attractive decorations for small fancies, slices, chocolates or desserts. The same ornaments may be piped with royal icing.

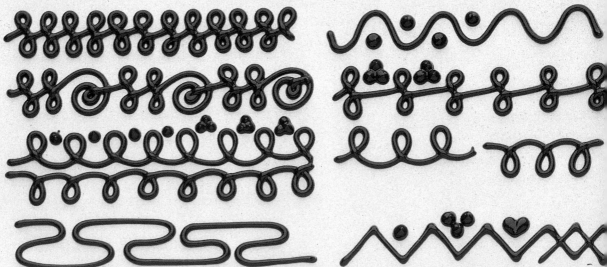

Chocolate ornaments for edging torten or for petits fours
* Silicone-coated paper avoids any possibility of the piped items sticking.

Piped chocolate ornaments for torten, petits fours or cream desserts

CHOCOLATE AND OTHER ICINGS

SPREADING COUVERTURE

Pour a little tempered couverture on to a sheet of greaseproof paper and spread it evenly with a palette knife. A little coloured sugar may be sprinkled on it while it is still liquid. Leave until set but not brittle. It may now be cut into shapes with a knife or fancy cutters.

SHAPES CUT OUT WITH CUTTERS

The cutter should always be dipped in hot water for a moment before use. Cut out the ornaments carefully. Wait until the couverture has set hard before breaking the cut-outs away. There are standard cutters with various motifs. They may be used for chocolate couverture, marzipan, truffle and aspic jelly.

SHAPES CUT WITH A KNIFE

Pour the tempered couverture on to a sheet of greaseproof paper. Spread it with a knife or palette knife to a thickness of about 3 mm (⅛ in) and leave in a cool place until set. Cut into geometric shapes as desired with a knife which has been warmed for a moment over a flame or hotplate.

Cutting shapes with a knife

Cutting out with cutters

Petits fours with piped chocolate ornaments and ice bombe decorated with buttercream and with cut-out and piped chocolate ornaments

Combinations of marzipan decorations and royal icing for various occasions. Petits fours covered with chocolate icing and decorated with ornaments of royal icing; below, buttercream roll with dots of buttercream and chocolate cut-outs

141

MARZIPAN

RAW MARZIPAN

Marzipan which is on sale
ready-made, known as "raw
marzipan", consists of two
parts sweet almonds and one
part sugar. For use in
decoration it may be mixed
with an equal amount of
finely sieved icing sugar, but
in any case a minimum of 50 g
(1¾ oz) icing sugar is required
for 100 g (3½ oz) raw
marzipan.

N.B. Marzipan quickly dries
out when mixed with icing
sugar. Consequently, only the
required amount should be
prepared at any one time and
quickly used.

COLOURED MARZIPAN

To colour marzipan, flatten it
with the ball of the hand and
place the food colour or a
little cocoa powder in the
centre. Now fold the sides
over towards the middle and
knead lightly until evenly
tinted.

TOOLS

The knife, various small
cutters and special wooden
modelling tools are used for
decorative marzipan
modelling.

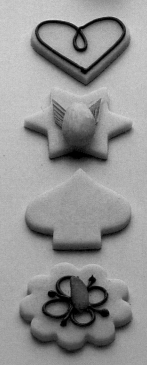

CUT-OUTS

To cut out shapes with various cutters, the marzipan which has been mixed with icing sugar is rolled out to a thickness of about 4 mm ($\frac{1}{5}$ in). To prevent it sticking, the working surface is lightly dusted with icing sugar; flour should never be used for this purpose. The same cutters may be used as for chocolate ornaments (see p. 136).

MARZIPAN ANIMALS

The body is modelled with a small roll of marzipan 5 cm (2 in) long and 1 cm ($\frac{3}{8}$ in) thick. For the legs 1 cm ($\frac{3}{8}$ in) cuts are made in the body at the back and front. For the head a piece of marzipan is rolled into a pear shape or a ball. The separate parts are stuck together with sugared water.

CAT

Lightly cut slits in the front paws to make claws. Shape the head round and use almond slivers for the ears, chocolate vermicelli for the eyes and whiskers, and red marzipan for the nose and tail.

HARE

A pear shaped head is modelled and cuts are made with a pair of scissors to hold the ears. Dots of piping chocolate are used for the eyes. A piece of angelica or candied orange peel is cut to make the tail. Two half almonds are inserted for the ears.

MOUSE

For the body a small roll of marzipan about 5 cm (2 in) long and 1 cm ($\frac{3}{8}$ in) thick is modelled to a pear shape. The eyes are dots of piping chocolate. The mouth and tail are made with red marzipan.

Cutting out

Separate parts modelled with marzipan for various animals – cat, hare, mouse

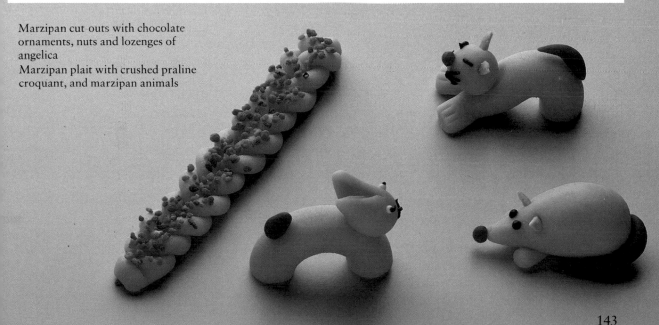

Marzipan cut-outs with chocolate ornaments, nuts and lozenges of angelica
Marzipan plait with crushed praline croquant, and marzipan animals

143

MARZIPAN

WIDE CONE

Cut out a disc of marzipan with a fluted cutter. Make a cut in it with a knife as far as the centre, then overlap one cut edge over the other and twist into a wide cone. Decorate with a walnut.

POINTED CONE

Cut out a disc of marzipan with a fluted cutter. Starting in the centre, cut away a triangle, then overlap one cut edge over the other and twist into a pointed cone. Fill with buttercream and decorate with a glacé cherry.

ROSE

For the heart of the rose a small ball of marzipan is shaped into a pointed cone. For the petals seven to nine small pieces of marzipan are each moulded into a ball about 1 cm ($\frac{3}{8}$ in) across, then placed on a surface which has been dusted with icing sugar. The ball is pressed flat with the finger, then the outside edge is gently stretched with the finger or a palette knife to make a thin petal. Each one is wrapped round the cone of marzipan separately so that one overlaps another and pressed in position. Finally the rose is cut off the base.

LEAVES

The marzipan is rolled out to a thickness of about 4 mm ($\frac{1}{5}$ in) and cut into leaf shapes with a knife. A cardboard pattern may be made as a guide. A knife is used to mark in the veins. Each leaf is then laid over the handle of a wooden spoon and lightly reshaped. Other leaf shapes may be made by cutting out marzipan discs with a fluted cutter and pressing the two halves together with a little egg white.

FLOWER

Using yellow marzipan, cut out either nine round petals or one round one and eight oval ones. In either case two leaves and a stem are cut from green marzipan.

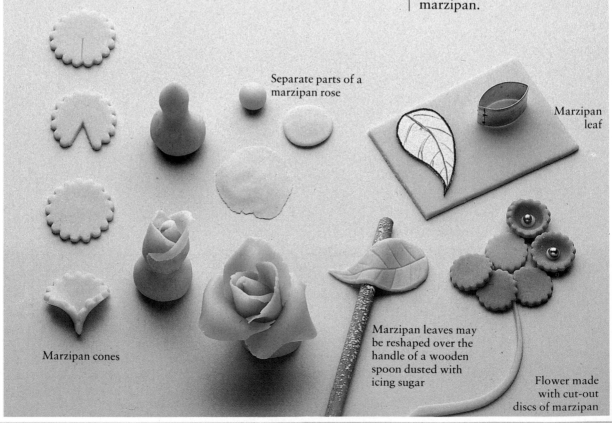

Separate parts of a marzipan rose

Marzipan leaf

Marzipan cones

Marzipan leaves may be reshaped over the handle of a wooden spoon dusted with icing sugar

Flower made with cut-out discs of marzipan

Various marzipan flower motifs suitable for edging or to decorate the centre of a torte or gâteau

MARZIPAN

CHRISTMAS TREE

The star is cut out with an appropriate cutter. The tree is first drawn on cardboard, then cut out. This pattern is placed on the marzipan which has been rolled out 4 mm ($\frac{1}{5}$ in) thick, and the outline of the tree is followed. The candles consist of oblongs topped with flames of coloured marzipan. The stand for the tree is half a fluted disc of marzipan.

BOOK WITH INSCRIPTION

The book is first drawn on cardboard and cut out. This pattern is placed on the marzipan which has been rolled out about 4 mm ($\frac{1}{5}$ in) thick and the outline is followed with a pointed knife. The book is decorated with a cross and candle. The scroll for the inscription is cut out with two plain cutters of different sizes. The resulting circle is cut in half and the ends are cut into two points.

GOOD LUCK CHARMS

The horseshoe is cut out of a strip of marzipan about 8 mm ($\frac{1}{3}$ in) thick. The dice are cut out as cubes measuring the same as the thickness of the marzipan. The dots are piped icing.
The snowman consists of two balls of different sizes. The arms are small rolls of marzipan. The hat is modelled with a small cylinder of marzipan, which is pinched between thumb and forefinger to make the brim. The nose is

The Christmas tree and book are cut out of rolled-out marzipan

Christmas tree pattern

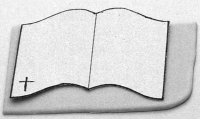

Book pattern

Scroll

Many shapes may be made with different thicknesses of marzipan

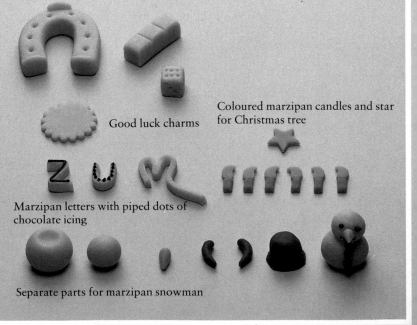

Good luck charms

Coloured marzipan candles and star for Christmas tree

Marzipan letters with piped dots of chocolate icing

Separate parts for marzipan snowman

yellow marzipan, the buttons and eyes are coloured marzipan.

INSCRIPTION

First a base is prepared. It may be a large cut-out disc or a scroll. For the letters, the marzipan is rolled out about 3 mm ($\frac{1}{8}$ in) thick, then cut into strips about 6 to 8 mm ($\frac{1}{4}$ to $\frac{1}{3}$ in) wide with the aid of a ruler and a plain pastry wheel. The strips are stood on edge and the numerals or letters are shaped, then cut off with a knife. The top of the letters may be further ornamented.

CANDLE

Marzipan candles may be made in many different ways with coloured marzipan. The candle itself is an oblong piece. The "halo" is a cut-out of untinted marzipan. The flame is cut from yellow marzipan.

Marzipan motifs for various occasions. The marzipan is rolled out to different thicknesses and cut with a knife or cutters. Additional effects are achieved by using coloured marzipan.

Zur 1. hl. Kommunion

Frohe Weihnachten

Icing Sugar and Cocoa Powder

Stripe Pattern

First cut six to eight strips of greaseproof paper about 1 cm ($\frac{3}{8}$ in) wide. They should be about 10 cm (4 in) longer than the diameter of the cake. Lay the strips on top of the cake zigzag fashion, parallel to one another or crosswise and dust the cake. Hold the strips by the ends and carefully lift them off the cake without spoiling the design.

Leaf Pattern

A particularly attractive pattern may be made with small, pressed well formed leaves and flowers which are placed on the cake before dusting.

Other Patterns

Other patterns, such as circles, spirals, diamonds or small fancy shapes, may be cut out of greaseproof paper and placed on a cake before dusting.

Tools

A pair of scissors is used to cut the patterns. Fine hair sieves are used to dust the cake evenly with icing sugar or cocoa powder.

Delicate designs may be created on cakes and dessert creams by dusting them with icing sugar or cocoa powder with the aid of paper patterns or cleaned leaves

149

Commercial Cake Decorations

Marzipan Fruits

These are tinted with food colours and used to decorate torten and gâteaux.

Sugar Sprinkles (Non Pareils)

Sold as strands or hundreds and thousands. They are suitable for decorating desserts, small cakes and fancies, and chocolate ornaments.

Fruit Jellies

These sugar decorations have a soft, elastic consistency. They can be used to make attractive patterns on large and small cakes or desserts.

Dragees

These are small, shiny, coloured, sugar-coated sweets, often silver or gold, suitable for decorating cakes and gâteaux for very special occasions, such as wedding cakes.

Sugar Flowers

Hard flower shapes made of sugar. They are sold in various sizes and colours and are very popular cake decorations.

Ready-made Chocolate Ornaments

They are used to decorate torten and gâteaux, large and small cakes and fancies, and desserts.

Candied Fruits

Candied fruits such as whole cherries or orange slices are suitable for decorating cream slices and cream torten or gâteaux.

Biscuits with candied fruit and sugar flowers

Cakes in unusual shapes, which are highlighted by colourful decorations

151

RECIPES

Unless otherwise stated, the quantities given are for 4 persons.

CHOUX PASTRY FILLINGS

BASIL CHEESE CREAM

200 g (7 oz) double cream cheese; 2 tablespoons tomato purée; 4 tablespoons white wine; $\frac{1}{2}$ bunch basil; salt, pepper; pinch of sugar; few drops lemon juice; few drops Worcester sauce
1. Place the cream cheese in a bowl and crush with a fork.
2. Add the tomato purée and wine and blend to a smooth cream.
3. Pick over the basil, wash it, then chop finely and mix with the cheese cream.
4. Add salt, pepper, sugar, lemon juice and Worcester sauce to taste.

ROQUEFORT CHEESE CREAM

100 g ($3\frac{1}{2}$ oz) Roquefort cheese; 250 g (9 oz) skimmed milk soft cheese (quark); 3 tablespoons slightly soured cream; salt, pepper; few drops Worcester sauce; few drops lemon juice; few drops cognac
1. Place the Roquefort in a bowl and crush well with a fork.
2. Add the quark and cream, then beat to a smooth cream.
3. Add salt, pepper, Worcester sauce, lemon juice and cognac to taste.

MUSTARD CREAM

1 pot ($\frac{1}{2}$ pt) slightly soured cream; 2 tablespoons medium mustard; 2 tablespoons fruit vinegar; 1 tablespoon lemon juice; salt, pepper, pinch of sugar; few drops cognac
1. Blend the cream with the mustard in a bowl. Add the vinegar and lemon juice and whisk to a foam.
2. Add salt, pepper, sugar and cognac to taste.

COCKTAILS

DUBLIN BAY PRAWN (SCAMPI) COCKTAIL

12 Dublin Bay prawns; various exotic fruits; 8 tablespoons yoghurt or slightly soured cream; Garnish 8 asparagus tips; 4 slices olive; leafy salads for decoration
1. For each cocktail, cut up two prawns and use a third one for decoration.
2. Peel the fruit and cut into bite-size pieces.
3. Mix the cut-up prawns and fruit together and fold in 2 tablespoons yoghurt or cream for each cocktail.
4. Fill into cocktail glasses and decorate with asparagus tips, sliced olive, chicory, red oak leaf lettuce and a wedge of lemon.

MARINATED LOBSTER ON MIXED SALAD LEAVES

500 g (1 lb 2 oz) lobster meat, cut up; 2 cl (1 fl oz) cognac; pinch of salt; 75 g (3 oz) boletus mushrooms, sliced; 100 g (3½ oz) leafy salads (red oak leaf lettuce, lamb's lettuce, radicchio, Belgian endive); 100 g (3½ oz) fruit (kiwi fruit, melon balls, tangerine sections, pineapple); 2 tablespoons tarragon vinegar; 2 tablespoons sesame oil; 320 g (11 oz) cocktail sauce (commercial); 2 cl (1 fl oz) amaretto;

Garnish asparagus tips, cress

1. Marinate the lobster in the cognac seasoned with the salt.
2. Arrange the mushrooms, salads and fruit decoratively on plates.
3. Sprinkle the salads with the vinegar and oil and season lightly with salt.
4. Divide the lobster between the plates, arranging it on the salads, and coat with the cocktail sauce which has been flavoured with amaretto.
5. Decorate with asparagus tips and cress, and serve.

KING PRAWNS IN MELON

12 King prawns each weighing 60 g (2 oz); 2 cl (1 fl oz) cognac; pinch of salt; 100 g (3½ oz) mixed fruit (melon balls, kiwi fruit, pineapple); 75 g (3 oz) mushrooms, sliced; 350 g (12 oz) cocktail sauce (commercial)

Garnish 2 medium melons (Ogen or Galia); 1 large kiwi fruit; mixed salad leaves; 12 white asparagus tips; sprig of dill

1. Prepare the prawns, set aside the three choicest ones for decoration and cut them in half lengthwise. Cut up the remaining ones finely and marinate in the cognac seasoned with a little salt. Add the fruit and mushrooms and mix well with the cocktail sauce.
2. Cut the melons in half and remove the seeds with a tablespoon.
3. Cut the melon flesh away from the skin with a grapefruit knife, then cut into eight pieces in a star pattern. Leave these in the melon shell.
4. Fill with the lobster and garnish with salad leaves, alternating dark and light coloured leaves. Place two asparagus tips on top.
5. In addition, the melon may be decorated with melon balls round the edge and a sprig of dill.

RECIPES

SCAMPI COCKTAIL

250 g (9 oz) scampi (frozen);
pinch of salt; 2 cl (10 oz)
cognac; 75 g (3 oz)
mushrooms; 100 g (3½ oz)
mixed fruit (melon balls,
pineapple, peach or
tangerine); 320 g (11 oz)
cocktail sauce (commercial);
<u>Garnish</u> 1 bunch dill; 6 stuffed
green olives; 60 g (2 oz)
horseradish cream; 1 lemon
1. Always thaw frozen
scampi in cold water. When
thawed, squeeze dry between
the hands.
2. Place the scampi in a bowl
and mix with a pinch of salt
and the cognac. Cover and set
aside for about two hours.
3. Reserve six choice scampi
for the garnish.
4. Add the remaining
ingedients to the rest of the
marinated scampi and mix
well.

5. For each portion, prepare a
cocktail glass with a sugar
frosted rim (see p. 120).
Divide the scampi salad
evenly between the glasses.
6. Using a savoy bag fitted
with a plain tube, pipe a fairly
large bulb of horseradish
cream on top of the scampi
salad and place one of the
reserved scampi on top.
7. The garnish consists of a
sprig of dill and two slices of
olive. A wedge or slice of
lemon is hung on to the rim of
the glass sideways for final
decoration.
8. In addition, a dark leaf of
red oak leaf lettuce or
radicchio and a light coloured
curly lettuce or endive leaf
may be placed in each glass.

<u>N.B.</u> When using lettuce or
endive leaves as a garnish,
dark and light ones should be
alternated to provide a
contrast.

ASPARAGUS COCKTAIL

360 g (12 oz) cocktail sauce
(commercial); 1 kg (2 lb 4 oz)
fresh asparagus; a few dashes
tabasco; a small jar mango
chutney or mango slices; 6
cocktail cherries with stalks;
various salad leaves as
decoration
1. Place two tablespoons
cocktail sauce in the bottom
of each glass.
2. Cut the asparagus spears,
which have been peeled and
cooked, into three pieces and
divide them evenly between
the cocktail glasses with the
tips on top.
3. Garnish each glass round
the edge with alternating dark
and light coloured lettuce and
endive leaves to form a
contrast. Place a little mango
chutney or a slice of mango on
the asparagus and decorate
with a cocktail cherry.

Fillings for Eggs

Filling 1

4 mushrooms; 1 slice cooked ham; 1 shallot; 2 stuffed green olives; pinch of salt; pepper, freshly ground; 1 tomato for 6 tomato leaves

1. Slice the mushrooms and set aside the eight best slices for the garnish.
2. Cut the ham and the rest of the mushrooms into strips. Dice the shallot finely.
3. Cook the shallot gently in a little oil in a small frying pan until transparent. Add the mushrooms and ham, mix and continue cooking gently until well blended. Season with pepper and salt, then leave in a cool place.

Filling 2

1 leek; 1 shallot, finely diced; 16 scampi; 2 black olives; juice of half a lemon; pinch of salt; pepper, freshly ground

1. Set aside a leek leaf with a very fresh-looking green top. Cut the rest into strips. About two heaped tablespoons of these are required.
2. Bring a small pan of salted water to the boil, add the leek leaf which has been set aside, cook until tender, then refresh in cold water. Cook the strips of leek in the same way for one minute, refresh in cold water, then drain in a colander.
3. Place the strips of leek in a bowl and add the diced shallot.
4. Select the four choicest scampi and reserve for the garnish. Cut the remaining ones in half if necessary. Mix with the strips of leek and add lemon juice, salt and pepper to taste.

Filling 3

4 slices smoked salmon; 1 shallot, finely cut; 1 small jar caviar; juice of half a lemon; oil; pepper, freshly ground

1. Roll up each slice of smoked salmon tightly and trim to a length of 3 to $3\frac{1}{2}$ cm ($1\frac{1}{4}$ in). Set aside for the garnish.
2. Mix the trimmings with the shallot and a little caviar, and add lemon juice, oil and pepper to taste.

Filling 4

8 choice anchovy fillets; 1 shallot, finely cut; 1 jar capers; 1 bunch chives

1. Select the four best anchovy fillets and reserve for the garnish.
2. Cut up the remaining fillets finely and add the shallot, together with capers and finely cut chives to round off the flavour. Season with a little salt if required.

Place the hollowed-out egg white halves on a plate and stuff with fillings 1 to 4, then pipe egg yolk paste on top.

RECIPES

GOOSE OR CHICKEN LIVER PASTE

50 g (2 oz) goose or chicken liver cream (canned); 30 g (1 oz) soft butter; cognac or other brandy; pinch of salt
1. Whisk the goose or chicken liver cream with the butter, brandy and salt until light.
2. Fill into a savoy bag fitted with a star (or plain) tube.
3. Pipe rosettes on to the medallions and decorate.

MEAT GLAZE

100 g (3½ oz) roast gravy; ¼ teaspoon aspic powder or ¼ sheet gelatine
1. Mix the gravy and aspic powder together in a small pan and stand aside for about 5 minutes.
2. Bring to the boil while stirring constantly.
3. Cool, then brush on to the medallions.

HOLLANDAISE SAUCE

6 egg yolks; 1 cup white wine; a few drops lemon juice; a few drops Worcester sauce; 250 g (9 oz) butter (hand hot); salt, white pepper
1. Mix the egg yolks with the wine in a fireproof basin.
2. Add the lemon juice and Worcester sauce to taste and whisk over a pan of hot water to a thick creamy consistency.
3. Remove from the heat and carefully stir in the butter drop by drop.
4. Season to taste with salt and white pepper and serve with asparagus.

REDCURRANT JELLY AND MINT JELLY

200 g (7 oz) redcurrant jelly; 200 g (7 oz) mint jelly; 40 g (1½ oz) aspic powder
1. For each of the two types of jelly, soak 20 g (¾ oz) aspic powder in 3 tablespoons cold water.
2. Add a heaped tablespoon of the jelly and transfer to a pan. Dissolve while stirring slowly. If the mixture is stirred too quickly it will become frothy.
3. As soon as the aspic powder is dissolved, add the remaining jelly and dissolve.

N.B. If the mixture does become frothy, a paper napkin is placed on the jelly and then lifted off, taking the froth with it.

CHEESE HEDGEHOG

1 loaf about 25 cm (10 in) long; 1 piece aluminium foil 30 × 40 cm (12 × 16 in); 30 2½ cm (1 in) cheese cubes; 30 cocktail sticks; 6 mandarin sections (or grapes or melon balls); 6 cherries (or radish roses); 6 stuffed olives; 6 pineapple chunks (or cherries); 6 silverskin onions (or gherkins or white radish balls)

1. Cut the loaf to the shape of a hedgehog with a knife, removing a wedge on the left and right from one of the long sides. Wrap the loaf in foil.
2. Impale the cheese cubes on the cocktail sticks together with the different garnishes and insert into the loaf in rows.

N.B. A pumpkin, cabbage or melon may be used instead of a loaf.

HERB CHEESE BALLS

400 g (14 oz) double cream cheese; 1 onion, very finely chopped; 2 tablespoons each parsley, chives, tarragon, lemon balm; 1 clove garlic; $\frac{1}{2}$ teaspoon salt; white pepper; a few drops lemon juice; a few drops brandy; 100 g (3$\frac{1}{2}$ oz) pumpernickel, finely grated
1. Place the cream cheese in a bowl and mash with a fork.
2. Add the onion and herbs.
3. Pound the garlic with the salt and add to the cheese, together with pepper, lemon juice and brandy to taste.
4. Moisten the hands and mould the cheese mixture into small balls.
5. Spread the pumpernickel crumbs on a plate and roll the balls in them.

CHESTNUT PUREE

500 g (1 lb 2 oz) fresh chestnuts; $\frac{1}{2}$ l (approx. 1 pt) salted water; $\frac{1}{2}$ cup slightly soured cream; 2 tablespoons fruit vinegar; 1 teaspoon lemon juice; salt, white pepper; a few drops Worcester sauce
1. Cut a cross in the chestnuts with a sharp knife.
2. Heat the water and boil the chestnuts until they may be easily skinned.
3. Remove, drain on a cloth, then skin.
4. Pound the chestnuts to a purée.

5. Place the cream, vinegar and lemon juice in a bowl and beat until light. Season well with salt, white pepper and Worcester sauce and carefully fold in the chestnut purée.

CRANBERRY CREAM

100 g (3$\frac{1}{2}$ oz) fresh cream; 100 g (3$\frac{1}{2}$ oz) cranberries; 1 cl ($\frac{1}{2}$ fl oz) kirsch; 1$\frac{1}{2}$ sheets gelatine
1. Lightly whip the cream, which has been well chilled, and fold in the cranberries. Gently stir in the kirsch.
2. Soak the gelatine in cold water for about 5 minutes, remove and squeeze gently.
3. Place the gelatine in a cup and dissolve over hot water.
4. Carefully blend the dissolved gelatine with the cranberry cream while stirring with a whisk.

N.B. If desired the cranberries may be sieved before use.

RECIPES

HAM BUTTER

70 g (2½ oz) cooked ham; 50 g (2 oz) butter; pinch of salt; pinch of sugar; black pepper, freshly ground; a few drops aquavit

1. Mince the ham twice and mix well with the butter which has been softened. Whisk to a creamy consistency.
2. Season to taste with salt and black pepper, and flavour with a small dash of aquavit.
3. Fill the ham butter into a savoy bag fitted with a large plain pipe.

HORSERADISH CREAM

50 g (2 oz) fresh horseradish; juice of 1 lemon; 2 cups stiffly whipped cream; salt; white pepper, freshly ground; pinch of sugar

1. Scrape the horseradish and grate very finely. Sprinkle at once with lemon juice.
2. Carefully fold into the whipped cream. Add salt, white pepper and sugar to taste.

TARTAR STEAK

180 g (6 oz) steak mince; 1 egg yolk; salt; pepper, freshly ground; paprika; onion, chopped

1. Combine the minced meat with the egg yolk, onion and seasonings to give a hot, spicy flavour.
2. Shape evenly into six balls and flatten a little. Using the back of a knife, decorate with a diamond pattern.
3. Place on the prepared bread bases and decorate.

WALDORF SALAD

400 g (14 oz) celeriac; 2 apples; juice of 2 lemons; 1 pot (½ pt) slightly soured cream; 4 tablespoons mayonnaise; salt, pepper; pinch of sugar; 3 cl (1 fl oz) brandy; 50 g (2 oz) walnut halves

1. Clean the celeriac, slice thinly, then cut into wafer-thin strips.
2. Peel and core the apples, then cut into thin strips.
3. Sprinkle the celeriac and apples at once with lemon juice and mix together in a bowl.
4. Whip the cream and mayonnaise together until light. Add salt, pepper and sugar to taste, and flavour with brandy.
5. Dress the salad with the cream mayonnaise, adding a few chopped walnut halves.

INDEX

A
Almond balls   52
Anna potatoes   54
Apple   34
Apples, coating   36
Apples for stuffing   36
Apples, poaching   36
Artichoke bottom   78
Artichoke bowl   78
Asparagus   74
Aspic, flowers under   110
Aspic for lining dishes   108
Aspic, working with   107
Aubergine   64
Aubergines for stuffing   72
Avocado   65
Avocados for stuffing   72

B
Banana   40
Banana boat   46
"Bethmännchen" potatoes   52
Bread baskets   92
Butter   96
Butter balls   98
Butter curls   98
Butter grapes   98
Butter reliefs   98
Butter rose   98
Buttercream, coloured   132

C
Candied fruits   150
Capsicum (peppers)   64
Carrot   51, 56
Carrot shapes   58
Carrot spiral   60
Celeriac   50
Celeriac shapes   58
Celery   74
Cherry tomato garnishes   66
Chocolate ornaments   138
Chocolate shapes   140

Choux paste shapes   94
Choux paste swans   94
Citrus fruit coronet   32
Citrus fruits, grooving   28
Citrus fruit water lily   31
Citrus fruit wedges   30
Courgette barges   84
Courgette bases   84
Courgette boats   84
Courgette turrets   84
Courgettes   80
Couverture   136
Croquettes   52
Cucumber   81
Cucumber balls   86
Cucumber boats   86
Cucumber coronet   86
Cucumber fan   84
Cucumber flowers   87
Cucumber grapes   87
Cucumber turrets   88
Cucumber wedges   86

D
Dill aspic   106
Dragees   150
Duchesse potatoes   54

E
Egg garnishes   102
Egg yolk paste   104

F
French buttercream   132
Fruit hedgehog   38
Fruit jellies   150

G
German buttercream   132
Globe artichoke   75
Gulls' eggs   100

H
Hens' eggs   100

J
Jelly glaze for fruit   106
Jelly oranges and lemons   33

K
Kiwi coronet   46
Kiwi fruit   40

L
Lemon   26
Lemon fan   28
Lemon wedges   30
Lily of the valley   104
Lime   26

M
Madeira aspic   106
Marzipan animals   143
Marzipan cones   144
Marzipan flower   144
Marzipan fruits   150
Marzipan leaves   144
Marzipan rose   144
Marzipan shapes   146
Melon   41
Melon coronet   48
Melon, stuffed   48
Melon with ball edging   48
Mushroom cap, grooved   91
Mushroom cap, turned   91
Mushroom caps, stuffed   91
Mushroom garnishes   90
Mushrooms   90

O
Onion flowers   62
Onion rings   62
Orange   26
Orange basket   32
Orange sections   30

P
Peach   35
Pear   34
Peppers for stuffing   70
Pickled cucumbers   84
Pickling onions   61
Pineapple   40
Pineapple arrangement   43
Pineapple boat   42
Pineapple, coating   44
Pineapple, stuffed   44
Potato and bacon cakes   54
Potato and cheese buns   54
Potato and cheese cakes   54
Potato balls   52
Potato mixture   52
Potato pear   52
Potato sausages   54
Potatoes   50
Presentation of cocktail titbits
   and canapés   114
Presentation of medallions and
   cocktails   118

Pumpkin   80
Pumpkins for stuffing   82

Q
Quails' eggs   100

R
Radish   51, 56
Radish flowers   56
Red onions   61

S
Shallots   61
Spanish onions   61
Spring onions   61
Sugar flowers   150
Sugar sprinkles   150
Sweet pepper shapes   70

T
Tangerine   26
Toadstool   68
Tomato   64
Tomato basket   68
Tomato coronet   68
Tomato flower   68
Tomato leaf   67
Tomato rose   67

W
White onions   61
White radish   51, 56
White radish spiral   60
White radish, stuffed   60

159

**British Library Cataloguing in
Publication Data**
Biller, Rudolf
    Garnishing and decoration.
    1. Cookery (Garnishes)
    I. Title   II. Garnieren und Verzieren
    English
    641.8′1   TX652

ISBN 0 900778 31 8